D0253034

Deer Hunting

Deer Hunting

TACTICS AND GUNS FOR HUNTING
ALL NORTH AMERICAN DEER

by

Norman Strung

J. B. Lippincott Company
Philadelphia and New York

U.S. Library of Congress Cataloging in Publication Data

Strung, Norman.
    Deer hunting.

    Bibliography: p.
      1. Deer hunting.   2. Deer.   I. Title.
SK301.S76   799.2′77357   73–4981
ISBN–0–397–00984–4

All photographs not otherwise attributed
are by the author.

This one's for the late Jack Barsness:
he was my mentor; he was my friend.

Preface

SINCE MAN FIRST LEARNED to use weapons, he has hunted to obtain food. Except in the remotest corners of the world, hunting is no longer necessary for survival, but a heritage stretching for aeons can't be denied by a paltry few centuries of "civilization."

Man will always be the ultimate predator. All of us live off lower forms of life. But because we have devised more efficient ways to produce food, sociologists and psychologists point out that man now sublimates: he transfers those energies once expended on hunting to comparable areas of intrigue such as business and athletics.

Well, most men do, and perhaps they lose something in the process. A few men, however, still become directly involved in their heritage through an exercise called deer hunting.

Deer hunting is not, as some critics claim, simply going out and shooting an animal. Neither is it truly "sport." Sport has the instant connotation of competition and, where nature is concerned, only a fool would offer contest. If anything, deer hunting is the opposite of these two common misconceptions. The "sport" is largely a matter of submission.

The successful hunter is neither combatant nor opponent, but one who has learned to be an observer and interpreter and a part of the natural world around him. He is immediately aware of a shift in the winds and the message they carry. He constantly notices details such as the rubs in slender saplings and knows the stories they tell about the activities of deer. He is a man who will feast on the musky-sweet smell of rotting leaves, the sparkling diamonds of frost on tall grass, and note where both have been disturbed by feeding whitetail.

To hunt a deer, you must first learn to move with the rhythm of nature, not of man. Therein lies the challenge, and a good deal of the worth, of deer hunting.

Another part of deer hunting's appeal lies in the fact that it is a rite. Again, critics claim that it is a masculinity rite, but I think they are wrong on that count too. Rather than a rite of manhood, deer hunting is a rite of man. In the shooting of a deer, man assumes and asserts his rightful place in the order of living things and, through the process of natural selection, ensures the excellence of deer as a species. In the squeeze of a trigger or the release of a bowstring lie both a touchstone and an affirmation of the basic, primal relationship between man and his environment.

There is a spiritual side to deer hunting as well. I have learned more religion in a cathedral of lofty pines than in any church, eating deer jerky by an altar of moss and sipping clear, cold springwater from a chalice of cupped hands. Yet eating a deer you shot isn't just symbol. Venison is also sustenance, a nourishing food that makes for delicious meals as well as a very real link between you and the infinite wonder that is the clockwork of the universe.

Deer hunting is more too, lots more, and like anything else of enduring value these things are impossible to pigeonhole, box up, or squeeze into a nutshell. It is enjoyment as diverse as understanding the principles of good game management and a poker game back at camp, as determining the age of a track and knowing how to make good mulligan stew—a complex combination of pragmatism and ritual, reason and emotion, work and reward.

It is in hopeful consideration, explanation, and appreciation of all these things that *Deer Hunting* is written.

Acknowledgments

A BLANKET THANK YOU goes to every one of the fish and game departments in the United States, Canada, and Mexico. Not only were they of immeasurable help by providing facts, figures, and fatherly advice during the writing of this book, but they are also the reason deer exist on the North American continent for the enjoyment of all.

Special awards for tolerance, interest, and patience beyond the call of duty go to the fish and game departments of Vermont, New York, New Jersey, Iowa, Oklahoma, Kentucky, North Carolina, Minnesota, Michigan, Idaho, Texas, Georgia, North Dakota, Utah, Arizona, and my home state, Montana.

And any acknowledgment list of this nature would never be complete without the names of Chris LoCascio, Tom Sicard, Eli Spannagel, Sr., Eli Spannagel, Jr., Dave Wolny, and the late Jack Barsness. Deer hunters and compadres all, they helped me learn to understand and love the outdoors and the creatures that dwell therein.

Contents

Preface   7

1. Deer Management   15

2. The Whitetail   67

3. Mule Deer   103

4. Skills, Savvy, and Equipment   135

5. Carcass Care   199

Epilogue   235

Bibliography   239

Deer Hunting

North Dakota Game and Fish Department

1
Deer Management

THERE WAS SURELY A TIME when deer on the North American continent enjoyed a purely "natural" existence, but it was far in the past, before the arrival of the Indian. In a primitive way, these first Americans "managed" their deer herds through the use of fire and its regenerative effect on forests.

With the coming of Europeans to this continent, more direct attempts at deer management were undertaken. Written records preserved from pre-Colonial days directed residents not to shoot deer at certain times, and limited them to a certain number of animals per family each year.

No less a historic figure than George Washington had a finger in the deer pie: Mount Vernon was maintained as a kind of "deer park" where Washington could watch the animals at his—and their—leisure. On a more massive scale, Theodore Roosevelt set aside a huge chunk of the Kaibab Plateau, part of which makes up the Grand Canyon, so the exceptionally large mule deer native to that region could forever be "preserved from the hunter's gun." These were all attempts by man to influence and control populations of deer—in other words, management.

Essentially, these are the same management techniques used today nationwide: habitat maintenance, hunting, and nonhunting.

Deer Hunting

When populations of deer become too great for the available food source, their numbers are reduced by hunting, resulting in a controlled harvest of surplus animals. When deer numbers are few and food plentiful, they are protected and allowed to reproduce, building up the size of their herd.

Ideally, this results in the optimum condition: a deer herd of sufficient size to utilize the available food, yet not so large that the deer pose a threat to agriculture, the environment, or themselves.

The net result of this "perfect" management is plenty of deer: deer to provide sport for the hunter, a snapshot for the photographer, and that indefinable something that comes over anyone who watches a herd of these animals graze their way into a gentle evening.

Simple? . . . Well, it could be.

The People Problem

John Renkavinsky stared out the window of his office at the heavy, wet snow streaming from the slaty sky. He took his pipe from his mouth just long enough to exhale a loud stream of air, then turned to face me.

"A book on deer management, huh?"

I shrugged my shoulders. "Well it's not all on management. Quite a bit will be devoted to hunting too, but I thought you might be able to give me some good leads."

John is an old friend of mine and Chief Wildlife Biologist for the Long Island division of the New York Department of Environmental Conservation—plainly put, a fish and wildlife man in a densely populated state. He pointed the stem of his pipe at me for emphasis.

"Norm, I'll give you current management thinking in a mouthful—reams of written prose in a sentence. Deer are easy to manage; it's the people that are hard."

His statement seemed cryptic at first, but as we jawboned away

16

that snowy January morning, a complex and slightly puzzling picture began to unfold.

Wildlife management, of which deer management is a part, is indeed a science. Its techniques and theories are based on observed, verified, and systemized data, and that data can be applied to making accurate predictions of future developments and trends in wildlife populations.

Because variables such as the weather, disease, and human population needs are somewhat unpredictable, wildlife management doesn't boast the unerring accuracy of the "pure" sciences, but basically an expert in deer management, working with accurate information, can forecast ups and downs in deer populations and, through manipulating causes, can scientifically control and manage the herd to produce optimum numbers of deer in balance with their environment.

Unfortunately and somewhat uniquely, however, laymen consistently debate the recommendations and conclusions of the wildlife biologist. It would be ultimate folly to argue with a chemist that hydrogen burned in the presence of oxygen won't create heat and water, or to tell a physicist that apples fall up, yet this is just the attitude commonly faced by fish and game departments across the country. Virtually anyone who has ever walked in the woods thinks of himself as a deer expert. And these "expert" opinions seldom agree with scientific fact.

To complicate matters more, fish and game departments in many states are organized and administered in such a way that they are politically sensitive. A state board of health can close down a restaurant for unsanitary conditions and few if any questions are asked. The public assumes that the board knows its business. But when game officials recommend a special antlerless deer season and produce scientific proofs to support their position, a hoopla usually results that resembles a major political campaign, with pro and con forces holding special meetings, circulating petitions, and attempting to force what is essentially a science to conform to a legislative process. The notion that the numbers and the activities of deer can be legislated is truly absurd.

The reason this hodgepodge of politics, public concern, and misinformation plagues our fish and game departments lies partially in our laws. Unlike Europe, where game is the property of the landowner, wildlife in America is public property owned by the people of a state. In other words, all of us—hunters and non-hunters alike—"own" our states' deer herds.

This notion of ownership, coupled with the public's divergent philosophies about what a deer should be and do, and liberally sprinkled with emotionalism, results in frequent public involvement unlike any other area of state/citizen administration. The briefest look at the types of groups that often become embroiled in deer management disputes should give some idea of the broad spectrum of motives and intent that fish and game departments must try to placate. They are enough to boggle the mind of the most astute public relations expert.

• Antihunters believe that management is wrong and should be banned. Their argument is largely emotional, based on the assumption that wildlife are somehow like humans and, if protected from the meddlings of man, will strike a balance with man and nature alike. Fact supports the opposite contention, but their antihunting emotional appeal is strong and popular among many people who are unfamiliar with natural order. It's easy to identify with anthropomorphized animals, and hold the hunter who stalks Bambi in contempt. Consequently, antihunting forces carry quite a bit of political clout.

• Landowners and agriculturists want deer managed because they often eat crops and ornamental shrubbery. However, many of these people are reluctant to allow hunters on their lands, fearing damage from that quarter. Although their numbers are small, their voice is loud, since they control the open lands on which deer exist.

• Lay conservationists and environmentalists exert influence too. While their concern with wildlife is legitimate and laudable, their information and facts are often faulty, resulting in vocal and strong support for seemingly noble, but wrong, causes.

• Hunters and sportsmen form the most powerful and active interest group influencing game management policies, and at first it would seem that the departments have at least one strong ally. Sadly, that isn't the case. By the weight of their numbers and organization, and by their failure to understand deer management needs, the hunting fraternity is often the most instrumental in creating and supporting policies unhealthy to deer populations.

The Stockpiling Syndrome

Deer hunters, antihunters, and conservationists, though frequently at odds, all want essentially the same thing: plenty of deer. To achieve this goal, they also agree on a plan of action in a very broad sense: less hunting, and hunting for bucks only.

Their thinking goes something like this: It's an established fact that a healthy deer herd will double itself in three years. Under extremely favorable conditions—plenty of food, a mild winter, and no predation by man or beast—a herd could conceivably double in two years.

When a hunter or wildlife buff spends a week in the woods and sees only a handful of does for his trouble, the solution seems obvious: curtail or wholly eliminate hunting for a number of years. Simple mathematics indicates that in six or seven years, there will be a deer behind every bush. This concept—leave them alone and they will multiply—is called stockpiling.

Hunting bucks only is a form of stockpiling too. Fawn crops run roughly 50–50, males and females. If you take only bucks, that leaves many more females to mate with polygamous males, theoretically creating that many more deer for next year.

Besides, no one wants does anyway. Whoever heard of mounting the head of a doe? What is more, many hunters are of the opinion that there is something inherently wrong with killing a doe—the weaker sex.

It all seems so simple, so obvious. Take just bucks, and when there aren't a lot of deer, leave them alone to grow. And that is often the position taken by individual sportsmen, conservationists, and their clubs across the country. When fish and game departments recommend just the opposite, public reaction is invariably strong.

"They're trying to kill off our deer." "Shoot a doe and you're killing two for next year." "There's plenty of food for the winter —the grass is hip-deep." "Save some for next year; we don't have enough now."

The cries go up at sportsmen's club meetings. Concerned nonsportsmen are enlisted for support. Editorials are written in newspapers. Public pressure mounts.

And usually, the recommendations of fish and game departments, backed by sound biological evidence, are compromised. A victory for sportsmen . . . for deer . . . ?

Hardly. Stockpiling as anything but an exceptional practice doesn't work. What is more, public insistence on stockpiling as a perpetual game management policy is the quickest way to destroy a healthy deer herd.

The Deer Cycle

When John Renkavinsky said, "Deer are easy to manage," he didn't mean simple. Deer, like squirrels, butterflies, beechnut trees, and babbling brooks, are part of a complex interrelationship we now call an ecosystem and a few years back called nature.

While it's true that left to her own devices nature will take care of her own, it isn't true that she will do it according to those plans man has found to be best. And I am not trying to be facetious; left to its pristine ways, a purely natural system can be monumentally uncompromising, wasteful, and cruel.

Deer Management

To see what I mean, let's pose a hypothetical situation. We shall begin with a hundred-acre island in the middle of a Northern lake and a "trapped" population of deer. Admittedly, we shall have to depend on some regularities that may not occur consistently in nature—an even distribution of sexes at birth in such a small sample, for example—but the principles the island will point up are perfectly valid.

"Deer Island" at first has an ideal environment for deer: woody, low-growing shrubs, small parks of grass, and scattered stands of tall, majestic timber—softwoods and hardwoods. The initial population consists of four healthy, mature deer: three does and a buck. Their first fall, they breed, and in the spring, as is normal with healthy females, the does drop two fawns each. The herd of four now stands at ten animals in the second year of their residence.

Any piece of land, be it an island, a farm, a county, or a state, has the capacity to produce just so much vegetation. Animals that feed on that vegetation are in turn limited by its production. In other words, you can't feed ten cows from a pasture that grows only enough hay for five, or a family of four on a garden that grows enough vegetables for two. This concept is called "carrying capacity."

So let's say that ten deer is the ideal carrying capacity of the island. With that number, there will be more than ample food during the warmer months, and just enough winter food in the form of buds, twigs, and woody plants (called browse) to see the whole herd through the colder months.

That fall, the deer breed again. Because the island's food supply is in good shape, the deer enter the critical winter months with a surplus of fat. There is enough winter browse to support them, so they emerge the next spring in excellent shape—lean, but healthy and strong. The three older does drop twins, and as is common with first births, the three-year-old does have one fawn each. All the young are strong and healthy too, well prepared to survive possibly adverse spring weather.

21

The herd of six does and four bucks has now grown to nineteen animals. They summer well, since there is still plenty of food during the warm growing months. When fall arrives, they are fat and sleek-coated, well prepared for the coming winter.

But the winter food supply isn't prepared for them. The critical browse is capable of supporting only ten animals, so when the snows get deep and times hard, the nineteen deer "overbrowse" the shrubs and woody plants that account for their winter food source.

"Overbrowsing" means eating so much of a particular plant that it is cut back to a point where the next summer's growth is retarded. This in turn means less food for the following winter than there was the year before. So even though by overbrowsing the nineteen deer winter well, they have done severe damage to the one thing that is critical to their survival: their food supply during the colder months.

The next spring, births are normal. The combined effect of fat from the summer before and overbrowsing has kept the herd healthy and they now increase their numbers to thirty-three.

At this point, the herd is in serious trouble. There is barely enough food to feed them in lush summer. They go into the winter without normal fat reserves. What little winter browse is available is decimated even before the harshest weather arrives.

Because there are no proper foods available, deer begin to eat anything to fill up their stomachs. They strip the bark off trees, girdling and killing them. They eat every twig they can find, chewing it back to thumb-thickness. They feed by standing on their hind legs and reaching for tree limbs until the island's vegetation develops a "browse line"—trees and brush stripped bare up to a height of 6 or 7 feet so that the whole area has the appearance of a pruned and manicured park.

And in their hungry search for food, they have changed the makeup of Deer Island. They have altered the growth of vegetation that other animals—grouse, squirrels, songbirds, and weasels

—depend on for survival. Perhaps saddest of all, the destruction they have caused hasn't helped them either.

Because their substitute foods have virtually no nutritional value, their health declines sharply. The effects of starvation begin to take hold, and the deer no longer have the strength in reserve to see them through periods of extreme cold weather and deep snow. By spring, half the herd is dead. Those that make it through the winter are pitifully emaciated. Fawn mortality rate is high; there are stillbirths, and fawns die in their beds because mothers can't supply milk.

Nature is beginning to take care of her own—to bring the herd back in balance with carrying capacity.

In their weakened state, disease and parasites are also prevalent. Even though food is rather plentiful in the summer, deer continue to die off until the herd is brought down close to its original level, but Deer Island can no longer carry ten animals. That critical winter browse has been so cropped, so decimated that the ideal number of deer on the island is now four. Still ten weak deer go into the winter, and continue to damage the winter browse, and continue to die. Then nature takes another step and lowers fertility rates: does drop only one fawn, sometimes none.

Over the years, a kind of balance is struck. Deer are small and scrawny in build; a 100-pound deer doesn't need as much food as a 200-pound deer. Bucks sport tiny, twiglike antlers, does drop single or no fawns, and mortality rates run 50 percent. Only a few fawns survive each year.

Then something happens to the vegetation. It may be a fire or a logging operation—perhaps some deadly disease that wipes out all but three deer. And the critical winter browse makes a comeback.

Food sources then exceed the needs of the deer, and with the available nutrition the condition of the resident deer improves. Fertility rates go up, racks get bigger, and then one spring there

Too many deer for the available food supply have overbrowsed their range. Note the "browse lines" on the trees. The deer have eaten everything they could reach by standing on their hind legs, creating a parklike effect.

is a herd of twenty deer on the island again—strong, heavy, healthy animals, ready to enter another winter with only enough food for ten. The cycle has come full circle, and the herd will once more be reduced.

Methods of Herd Reduction

Starvation is the end product of poor deer management or no management at all. If the range will not support the herd, and if the annual crop is not removed by hunting, starvation will remove it. This is an axiom, an unalterable rule in deer management.*

In my early teens and beyond, I was protégé and companion to a kind and patient compadre named Tom Sicard. Tom taught

* James G. Teer, *Texas Deer Herd Management.*

24

me a great deal about the outdoors, and though the cold of too many duck blinds and the wet of too many rains have finally bitten into his bones to a point where he can no longer hunt, we still see a lot of each other and I continue to learn at his hand.

In the green years of our companionship, we both loved deer hunting—not just shooting them, but stalking them to watch their activities at all times of the year. One of our favorite times was late winter, when animals were concentrated by deep snow, and slipping up on them with silent skis or snowshoes was easy.

One particularly bad year for the deer—deep and constant snow far into the spring—we eased up on a wintering herd and practically stumbled over a yearling doe bedded down in some juniper. That the deer was in bad physical shape was apparent, and it became more apparent as we stood there. The deer didn't have the strength to get to her feet.

I felt much as one would toward a stricken puppy—deep pity, with the wish that I could do something to help the animal. "Can we do anything?" I asked.

Tom nodded gently, took his hunting knife from his sheath, and cut the deer's throat.

The brutal fact of that act and its more brutal alternative have remained with me since. I am hardly a weeping romantic, but any notion that hunting and management should be eliminated in favor of "letting the deer take care of themselves" left my consideration that day. Starvation is an unspeakably cruel and wasteful method of herd reduction.

Predators are often pointed to as a means of control. Predators aren't feasible because those animals that would normally feed on deer—wolves, mountain lions, and occasionally bears—are hardly acceptable neighbors to modern civilization. The citizens of Westchester, New York, would not welcome the importation of puma to control their burgeoning whitetail herd.

Smaller predators—bobcats, lynxes, foxes, and coyotes—seldom kill deer unless they come upon a sick or extremely young animal. Tests have been made on the contents of their stomachs to support this contention; their primary food is rabbits and other rodents.

Incidental mortality certainly occurs. Deer become entwined in fences and starve, jam their heads or legs in the crotches of trees and can't pull free, fall off cliffs, die because they fall on slick ice and can't get to their feet, drown by falling through ice, and are swept under by spring-swollen rivers. Dogs—domestic pets—when allowed to run in packs take a considerable toll of deer. So do auto accidents and illegal poaching. But none of these factors add up to a number sufficient to compensate for the number of new deer that are born into a herd yearly. Only starvation or direct reduction through hunting can accomplish that.

Slaughter as a management tool is often suggested as a way to control numbers of deer that have grown beyond the ability of the land to support them. The vehicle most often suggested is a "group of trained marksmen."

This technique was once used on elk in Yellowstone National Park. Elk were herded by helicopter, then gunned down by the thousands, both from the air and by rangers posted on the ground.

The result was an unparalleled waste of meat—a matter of personal morality. The slaughter was extremely distasteful to the public, who raised a monumental outcry that eventually stopped it.

The slaughter also offended natural selection. In such a programed, mechanized kill, every animal caught up in the net was mowed down: the smart, the dumb, the strong, the weak, the healthy and the lame. This simply doesn't occur in nature. The best-equipped to survive always live, to reproduce and improve their kind. At the very least, it is unwise to tamper with natural order.

"Trained marksmen" are also rather ineffective in terms of deer. Elk are instinctive herd animals; they can be moved and cajoled into the open like so many cows. Deer are just the opposite; they will slip through a line of hunters and double back with will-o'-the-wisp magic. Theodore Roosevelt once tried a huge deer roundup in the Kaibab. His "deer park" in the Grand Canyon was being ravaged by the uncontrolled herd he had legislated into overpopulation, and he hoped to move them out to greener pastures. Hundreds of experienced cowboys beat through the brush in a well-organized drive—and didn't displace one deer. They all doubled back and returned to their original haunts.

This means, then, that in terms of deer control those "trained marksmen" would virtually have to function as lone hunters, killing one deer at a time. Obviously, this would be a year-round job, which raises the question of pay.

Deer are currently managed by fish and game departments, that are supported largely, not by public taxes, but by license fees collected from sportsmen. Without deer hunters to buy licenses, who would pay the salaries of the "marksmen"?

Of all the theories of deer control and herd reduction, there is only one practical alternative to out-and-out starvation: the citizen/hunter.

The Hunter and the Deer Cycle

"On a nationwide basis, the deer hunter is the most effective management tool available. More can be done to sustain the highest possible deer harvest through proper use of the hunter than by any other economically feasible management tool. Once a herd has reached carrying capacity, it must be controlled by adequate, either-sex hunting. If it isn't, nature will control it through disease, winterkill, starvation, lowered reproduction, or a number of other factors, and invariably at lower numerical levels than can be maintained through intelligent management."

The quote is from Gene Stout, a big-game biologist with the State of Oklahoma, and his words amount to a basic tenet of wildlife management. Elimination, removal, control, killing—

call it what you will—reduction of deer populations by hunting is the best route to maximum-sized herds of healthy deer in balance with their environment.

At face value, that position might seem hard to justify. After all, how can large-scale killing of deer benefit them?

To explain this, let us turn the clock back on Deer Island. There was a time, two years after the initial stocking of four deer, when nineteen healthy animals inhabited the place. Both they and their environment remained in balance up to the third winter—the time when nineteen deer browsed on vegetation that could support ten.

Instead of letting nature take her terrible course, let us now introduce man and his management techniques during the third summer, and have biologists inspect the island to determine herd size and the carrying capacity of the native vegetation.

There are many ways to make these determinations, and each "test" provides a cross-check on other results. For example, herd size and the relation of yearling to older deer can be measured by pellet groupings. This involves examination of the size, freshness, and frequency of deer droppings in proportion to the dimensions of the acreage studied. Tracks—their size, number, and freshness, again in proportion to acreage—provide another yardstick. Aerial surveys where numbers of deer are counted by sight is another possibility, and so are drives, where all the deer in a predesignated area are pushed past observers.

Carrying capacity of vegetation is even easier to determine. Biologists know exactly those plants utilized by deer in the winter (a deer's food preferences change with the season), and how much of them a deer needs for daily maintenance (about four pounds of air-dried food per hundred pounds of body weight).

Because they know those foods favored by deer at other times of the year, they can also, by surveying the current amount of vegetation being consumed, approximate the number of animals present and the amount of food they will need in the winter.

The hunter is the key to a deer herd in balance with its environment.

After all their tests are complete, the biologists then determine that winter forage on the island is capable of supporting ten deer through the winter *without suffering damage or retardation.* They also find that a total of nineteen deer now inhabit the island. Their recommendation, then, is that nine deer be removed from the island—that the herd be reduced by nearly one half.

Realize, too, that no matter how you juggle age and sexes, some of those deer harvested are going to be antlerless—does or fawns of either sex. A "bucks only" season would either wipe out all the breeding males or fail to bring the herd into balance with its winter browse.

Should the herd be precisely harvested according to recommendations (again, we are assuming quite a bit because of such a small sample), it would be possible to maintain an annual harvest of nine animals from Deer Island—a maximum yield.

But more important than any "meat produced" evaluation, the critical habitat and natural balance would be maintained from year to year, providing a maximum-sized, healthy herd of deer for the hunter and looker and a stable environment for other wildlife as well. None of these animals will ever have to experience the hunger, sickness, and starvation of "natural" self-elimination.

Of course, "Deer Island" is just an illustration. In larger, real-life deer herds, there are factors influencing stability and production beyond those outlined here. But in their recommendations, all these extraneous variables are taken into account. Yet all too often, the advice and predictions of wildlife professionals, based on sound, demonstrable evidence, are sadly ignored.

Vermont: The Decline and Fall of a Deer Herd
Vermont has long had a deserved reputation as a top place to down a trophy whitetail buck. In 1966 and 1967 the Green

Mountain State recorded both a deer harvest and a deer population density unequaled in conservation history. Yet today Vermont's whitetails and their future look bleak indeed.

The decline and fall of this great deer herd were tied directly to the "people problem" aspect of game management. Biologists correctly predicted disaster long before herds ever reached the critical stage in '66 (roughly comparable to "Deer Island" with a population of thirty-three animals). When overpopulation trends first began to develop, they came out in insistent favor of a large antlerless deer harvest, and their recommendations were ignored in favor of stockpiling.

To get the total picture, we have to begin in 1962. The state enjoyed a record harvest that year—over 12,000 deer. All signs pointed to a healthy herd, a stable herd. Winter range conditions were good, with critical feed in good supply.

Although an even bigger kill was forecast for 1963, it was never realized. Poor weather kept hunters home; noisy, crusty woods favored the deer. Only a little over 10,000 whitetail were harvested that year.

The situation wasn't of sufficient magnitude to be a problem. The herd had been underharvested, according to Fish and Game Department statistics, but minor underharvests had occurred before without trouble. However, data gathered then and from years past—weight, antler beam, age composition, and female fertility rates—all indicated a herd undergoing a change.

Basically, the change was in age composition. It appeared that young, year-and-a-half-old deer of both sexes had increased their relative populations dramatically over the past ten years. This meant a growing herd—more deer. Because of the increased numbers of animals, and the food they would need to survive, fish and game officials warned the sportsmen: if we have a mild winter, you can expect more deer next year. However, horns on buck deer will be smaller than they have averaged in the past, and weights will be lighter.

They also pointed out that imbalanced age distribution isn't good management. Since fawns are the most prone to winterkill, a herd with an overbalance of yearling deer could be severely decimated by a bad winter. They recommended a harvest of more antlerless deer to regain a proper balance.

Enough said—it was a casual warning, and largely ignored.

True to predictions, 1964 saw a record harvest of nearly 15,000 whitetail. The previous winter had been mild, and the hunting season favorable to the hunter.

The hunters were happy enough, but the Fish and Game Department noted smaller body and antler development in the deer taken from southern Vermont. Winter foods were getting scarce in that area when compared to the huge population of deer inhabiting the region. Although they still predicted that the herd would grow, and, allowing for a mild winter, would break previous record harvests, the Department saw fit to issue a stronger warning:

"The continued improvement of deer and the unprecedented herd growth we are presently experiencing in Vermont are *not* the result of improved habitat. They are the temporary by-product of two exceptionally temperate, back-to-back winters."

It is impossible to say exactly what the public pulse was like in Vermont in 1964. But it is easy to theorize. The Vermont herd was producing record numbers each year, and predictions were for even more deer the next year. What could possibly be wrong with that? "Leave 'em alone, let 'em grow. Soon we'll have a deer behind every bush." The Vermont Fish and Game Department's warnings were lost in the wilderness.

The year 1965 broke a record. A little over 16,000 bucks were taken. Still, the Fish and Game Department warned that "the '64–'65 wintering population was bolstered by 15,000 more deer than had ever yarded together on Vermont's overcrowded winter range."

They had figures to support a general downtrend in deer condition (weight, antler measurements, age composition, fertility).

A solution was needed now, before irreversible damage was done to browse and the herd itself. More deer had to be harvested, and not just bucks. To readjust the age-composition imbalance, large numbers of does and fawns had to be removed during the next season. They weren't. Sportsmen and the general public still refused to accept the notion of a large antlerless kill.

This Vermont buck would make any hunter more than happy, but he worried the Vermont Fish and Game Department. Reliable indicators, such as the rather spindly size of his antlers, pointed to a herd undergoing an explosion. "More deer must be harvested," the Department warned, "or you can expect fewer, not more, deer as well as an ecological and humane disaster."

John Hall, Vermont Fish & Game Dept.

Deer Hunting

The winter of '66 was unusually mild. Deer seemed to be everywhere and seriously harassed orchard and nursery owners. Spring counts of winter-killed deer revealed a significant jump in mortality rates, and every deer analyzed was found to be in poor nutritional condition at the time of death.

Predictions were for an even greater harvest in the fall of 1966. Nearly 20,000 deer! The Fish and Game Department finally received permission from the state legislature to step up antlerless kill, but public pressure limited the kill to not more than 5 to 8 percent of the total herd. It was too little and too late.

The 1966 Vermont Big Game Review and Forecast opened with a foreword by the Commissioner of the Fish and Game Department. Vermont, he stated, would have a herd of 250,000 deer by November of 1967. It was a turning point, for if the herd continued to grow unchecked, Vermont would be responsible for an unparalleled waste of deer.

The contents of the Big Game Review went on to support his warnings: they told of enormous crop and forest damage, the increasing waste of deer through winter mortality, and the gradual depreciation of their physical qualities.

In 1967 only 16,425 bucks were harvested. In general, they were small in frame and in antler structure. Long yearlings, who under healthful conditions grow two to six points by the middle of their second year, had spindly spikes. Seventeen percent of the yearling bucks were "baldies"—they didn't have legal-sized antlers.

The dead deer search the previous spring explained why.

• Classic starvation, where an unmolested animal simply lay down and died, was found in every county surveyed.

• In Vermont's southern counties, winter-killed animals averaged 18.7 per square mile of winter range!

The truly sad thing about all these useless deaths may not be immediately apparent. There is, of course, the very real loss—practical and humane—when any deer dies of starvation. But before that animal died, he consumed much now-wasted winter food. Had he been eliminated through hunting the previous season, he would have been "used," and would have afforded another deer more food to see it through the winter.

The estimates for the 1968 season predicted 15 to 20 percent fewer bucks in the woods than the previous year. Man had not done his job well enough, so nature was starting to bring things back into balance—and, by human standards, in a cruel, wasteful way.

The 1968 season saw a kill of 12,942 deer, down 21 percent from the previous year. Statistics indicated more physical deterioration within the herd. The Fish and Game Department predicted a gloomy outlook for the future: "The situation *will not* correct itself. Only public backing of sound management principles will." Even though the deer kill was down, large numbers of does and fawns had to be removed from the herd to bring it back in balance with the winter food supply.

The public responded to this plea in a predictably contrary way, and perhaps you can guess its attitude. The herd was down, laymen said, because of overhunting and the previous antlerless deer seasons. The solution to the problem was obvious: shorter, bucks-only seasons. Perhaps most shocking to common sensibility, these demands were made in the light of a verified figure of 20,000 deer dead from malnutrition and related causes that previous winter—a "natural" death rate that far exceeded the hunter-kill!

The outlook for the '69 season predicted deer harvests down again. They were, by 5.5 percent. Physical deterioration of the herd continued at a rapid pace. Seventy percent of all winter-killed deer were fawns. Again it was pointed out that if some of these animals had been taken the previous season, more deer would have been present in the fall. The percentage of young deer killed—an indication of herd composition—was way down. The herd was now in the opposite condition of what it had been in the healthy days of '63 and '64, with an unusually large number of older animals. The herd was shrinking.

In 1970 the buck harvest declined 21 percent from the previous year to 9,680 males, the lowest Vermont harvest since 1956. The reason was that 30,000 deer had died during the previous winter.

The Vermont Fish and Game Department produced volumes of statistics to support their contention that if the deer herd was to improve, more, not fewer, deer of both sexes needed harvesting.

• During a four-winter period, deer losses from winterkill totaled a staggering 112,800, nearly double the firearms kill!

• The hypothetical "average" Vermont doe was in poor health, weighed 100 pounds, and produced one fawn. Healthy, robust does average 130 pounds and normally produce two fawns.

• Of the fawns entering winter yards, 50 percent were not expected to live to see spring.

• Winter forage plants were close to the point where they may *never* recover normal growth.

The public response was sad, but predictable. The bill that had allowed the Vermont Fish and Game Department to hold limited either-sex hunting (5 to 8 percent of the herd, when permission for 20 percent reductions had been asked for) was not renewed in 1971.

In their "outlook for 1971 and beyond," the Fish and Game Department flatly stated that the state's overbrowsed deer yards could no longer support the numbers of deer sportsmen had known in the past. Their predictions continued to forecast physical and numerical deterioration until such a time as balance could again be achieved through intelligent management. The tone of their statement was one of frustration and defeat. They had tried to maintain a magnificent herd and had lost.

Deer Management

Managing the Hunter: Laws and Seasons

Hunters and hunting were the most logical answers to Vermont's problems, but even though the hunter is the best tool at the biologist's disposal, merely turning him loose in the fall woods isn't enough to fulfill many of the precise needs of management.

More direction, more control over the function of the hunter are needed to get those specific results often required to achieve a balanced herd. For example, the deer in the southern part of a state might have experienced a mild winter and risen in population. In the northern counties, a freak ice storm or a late spring blizzard could have reduced deer numbers. A wooded area near a large city might have a herd of deer so large that they have been destroying the ornamental shrubbery of suburbia, and an intensively farmed area a few miles beyond those woods could have so little escape cover that the deer living there might conceivably be wiped out by heavy hunting.

The end result of poor management is starvation; it is an axiom, and unalterable rule.

John Hall, Vermont Fish & Game Dept.

These diverse circumstances simply can't be handled by one cover-all law such as a two-week either-sex season. Consequently, hunting seasons often arrive attached to a bird's nest of regulations that would confuse a Philadelphia lawyer.

While their complexities are sometimes maddening (and public-relations-conscious fish and game departments do take this into account when writing them), they are necessary. Why they are and how they work are best understood by examining several of the laws common to hunting and their potential effect on the hunter and the deer.

Seasons are the most common controls, but contrary to expectation length alone does not necessarily determine the size of the harvest. For example, a very short season—say one day—in a heavily forested area near a large city will usually produce a bigger kill than a long season. This is because many hunters can be counted on to be in the woods that one day, and game will have more trouble eluding human contact.

Rather than a long season's meaning the most hunting pressure, a long season tends to spread out that pressure. The 1,000 hunters who would plan to be in the woods on a one-day season are reduced to a handful a day when the season is a month long.

This, in turn, reduces the kill, since unskilled hunters are less likely to "luck into" a deer pushed out by another hunter, and truly "skilled" deer hunters make up a minority of the hunting public.

This same rule of thumb relating concentrations of hunters to big kills is reflected in the day on which the season is scheduled to open.

When opening day falls on a weekend, there will be many hunters in the woods at once, and a high initial kill. Schedule that first day for the middle of the week, and pressure is spread out. Dedicated deer hunters and those who have a day off will be there to hear the first shot, but more casual hunters won't pick up their guns until the weekend.

Although it may sound as if your chances are best when you

crush brush with a big crowd, this isn't so. More deer will be taken on a crowded opening day or weekend, but remember, more people are hunting too, so the ratio of successful to unsuccessful hunters is often lower than on days when the woods are not full of people.

Timing of the season means a lot as well. An early season means a low kill of bucks. At this time, they are largely solitary and sedentary, and excess foliage aids their concealment. An early "bucks only" season means a low harvest of deer, and an early "either-sex" season indicates a high harvest of antlerless deer.

A late season usually means a relatively high kill of bucks, since with the onset of rut they become more active and more prone to human contact.

Very late either-sex seasons are sometimes used when deer populations reach the danger level. The idea is to foil those hunters who insist on "holding out for a buck." If the season is late enough, bucks will have lost their horns, and without that identification virtually the entire harvest will be made up of does and fawns since bucks will by then again be solitary and secretive.

Weather is perhaps the most maddening factor game-lawmakers have to contend with, simply because of its unpredictability. Pleasant weather means that many hunters will enter the woods. To some extent, pleasant weather favors the deer, but still, those large numbers of hunters will cause a high kill. Nasty weather—particularly deep snow—means fewer hunters in the woods. Although fewer animals will be harvested, the percentage of hunters that score will rise because the weather now favors the nimrod.

Sex and bag limits are obviously control factors. A bucks-only limit will cause a herd to increase (remember, there are many other factors influencing this rule of thumb). A controlled harvest of antlerless deer will stabilize a herd or reduce its size, and so will an increase in bag limits.

The harvest of antlerless deer is a rather critical matter, since an overkill could severely affect next year's herd. Consequently, laws concerning antlerless hunting are often quite intricate, so that results can be counted upon to be rather precise.

Generally, these special laws fall into three categories: doe days, individual permits, and party permits.

Doe days—days during the season when any deer is fair game —have declined in popularity as a management measure, because they are imprecise. Because of the influence of some of those other factors discussed earlier—weather, terrain, etc.—doe days often result in an erratic harvest. Too many one year, too few the next. There is the safety factor too, the danger that an "if it moves, shoot it" attitude will develop on a special day when all deer are fair game for everybody.

Individual permits offer the apparent advantage of knowing just how many does will be harvested. It is great in theory, but not really in practice. Again, outside factors highly influence hunter success and participation, so a precise harvest is difficult to achieve.

Party permits seem to do the best job of turning out predictable results. Under this system, a predesignated number of hunters (usually two to four) apply for a "party" doe permit. Any of the four hunters can shoot the doe, but only one is allowed per party. Because there are four people looking for one doe, hunter success is quite high under this system. The number of permits issued comes quite close to the number of deer harvested, and management then becomes more precise.

Special post-season harvests are occasionally used in the West. As in any season, these are designed to keep herds in balance, but Westerners have a rather unique situation to contend with.

There, as anywhere else, the winter range is the critical factor. These are relatively small areas of brushy bottomland, in sharp contrast to summer ranges, which are almost too vast to comprehend.

When deer are spread out over their summer ranges, they are hard to find. And continued hunting pressure in the easy-to-reach lowlands will often keep them up there as long as the hunting season lasts.

So often, the season is closed, the winter migration to the low country is allowed to take place, then the season is reopened in selected areas to allow a proper reduction of the now concentrated and easier-to-hunt herd.

Because deer tend to remain in a general area and exhibit population trends unique to that area, many states use zoned hunting as a management tool. This amounts to laws of season and limit applied by region, giving management personnel a degree of flexibility.

A good example of how zoned hunting works can be found in the State of Montana. There, the zones run roughly along county lines and fall into two basic classifications: "A" tag and "B" tag areas.

After a yearly survey of the size of the deer herds and the available feed, the Fish and Game Department designated zones determined to have low populations of deer as "A" zones. In these areas, the hunter may shoot only one deer, and must then tag it with a special "A" tag that is part of the hunting license.

Areas with high populations of deer are designated as "B" zones, and in them the hunter may use either his "A" or "B" tag and can take up to two animals.

The net effect produced covers both harvest and hunting pressure. By virtue of the fact that an area is legal for both A and B tags, sportsmen know that there are plenty of deer and tend to hunt those zones the most. This system also makes available control by species. Many counties in Montana have a surplus of whitetail that hunters ignore. In these places, a whitetail harvest can be encouraged by making the "B" tag whitetail only, which the Fish and Game Department often does.

Deer Hunting

Laws and a Practical Problem

In 1972 Minnesota faced an uncommon problem these days: too many hunters and too few deer.

The situation resulted from an unfortunate combination of conditions and circumstances. As might be expected, lack of available winter feed played a major role in herd reduction. Six severe winters in a row compounded the problem. Then in 1970, when a short, two-day season produced far more hunters than were anticipated, the resulting unexpected overkill plummeted whitetail populations to the danger level.

Rather than cutting back the herd, Minnesota was faced with the atypical task of increasing its numbers. Part of their solution was to increase the quality of the habitat through forest management, a subject we shall discuss later. The other way they rectified the problem was through laws.

In 1971 they simply closed the season. The move was largely a stopgap measure, because even a severely depleted herd, left on its own in a poor environment, develops unhealthy characteristics of age structure. There was also the pragmatic matter of money. Deer don't pay salaries—sportsmen do; and without a deer season no licenses were bought.

Management and money both demanded some sort of season for '72, so Minnesota's Department of Natural Resources came up with a unique solution that satisfied everybody, including the needs of a deer herd that had to grow.

The entire month of November was open to deer hunting; however, each hunter was limited to a specific period of time for his hunt. If he wanted to hunt during the pleasant weather of November 1 to 15, he could choose any three consecutive days. If he preferred to hunt during the usually stormy last half of the month, he could have any five consecutive days. Because of this spreading out of hunting pressure, it was predicted that no more than 18,000 hunters would be in Minnesota's vast woods at any one time.

While this type of season offers everyone an opportunity to hunt, a light harvest should occur, giving the deer a chance to increase their numbers.

This new plan also benefits the Minnesota sportsman, since it means less competition, a longer season than he has enjoyed in the past, and the opportunity for a "quality hunt," a factor that is becoming an increasingly important ingredient in wildlife management.

Quantity Versus Quality

Historically, deer have been a source of food first and of relaxation second. Today, the view of deer as so much meat is becoming less and less important in the minds of sportsmen. Deer hunting is almost strictly a matter of recreation.

Since the public owns the deer, and recreation, not meat, is their interest in these animals, management personnel are vitally interested in defining the term "recreation" to the public's, and their, satisfaction. And it involves a lot more than a good dictionary.

Hunters want to be successful; they want to bring something home as tangible evidence of their adventure. In order to satisfy the most hunters, the herd must be managed for maximum production, with age groupings in favor of young animals. This is the way most states now manage their herds, for it also satisfies the nonhunting outdoorsman who has a better chance to enjoy seeing deer in the woods.

But hunters and hikers enjoy something else too: the sight of a magnificent horned buck. And while herds managed for horn production can be both stable and in balance with their environment, they won't be as big in numbers as one tailored to maximum meat production; they require more deer in older age groupings.

Sportsmen must then realize that they can't have their cake and eat it too. They can't have huge herds and huge horns, so they must choose which type of management they want. Personally, I would predict a gradual shift in the future to more emphasis on horns and less on meat.

One other aspect of quality that has raised some current speculation in management is the hunt itself. True, the primary goal of a deer hunt is downing an animal, but there are ancillary benefits that in total might be far more important and meaningful than shooting a deer.

Surely, some computerized analyst is going to figure out how to define and measure them, but I just call them things like the hoot of an owl, the unbelievable blackness of a night far removed from city lights, and the stark beauty of being blessedly alone in a quiet woods.

These pleasures are becoming increasingly more difficult to enjoy as the ranks of hunters swell and open lands shrink each year. In the future, we may well find Minnesota's temporary solution common practice across the nation—and be thankful for it.

Habitat Management

The world that exists beyond the confines of pavement and groomed lawns is vibrant, dynamic, and always changing. Trees grow old, die, and rot, and new growth takes their place. Game animals live and die, and are in turn replaced by their offspring. The entire scheme of this wild world is interrelated and infinitely complex, and it isn't static. Subtle changes occur every day, and in thirty years that patch of woods you remember hunting as a kid is a strange and alien territory.

The job of deer management is, then, also tied to forest management, because, like deer, forests undergo cycles with a direct influence on the wildlife that live within their borders.

Wildlife need two things to exist: food and escape cover. In terms of deer, food isn't just anything that grows; they are extremely selective feeders, preferring those plant types that grow best in open sunlight.

Cover to a deer means natural growth that protects the animal from detection and the weather—in other words, medium to large stands of timber.

Where both proper food and sufficient escape cover exist simultaneously, deer will thrive so long as their numbers are kept under control. However, this optimum balance of lots of food and good cover doesn't last forever because forests change their makeup.

The classic example of how a forest changes over the years begins with fire that rages through a stand of virgin, cathedral-like timber.

There are, indeed, an almost tangible peace and tactile beauty about a stand of ages-old trees that reach the sky. But in terms of most forms of wildlife, that forest is dead. The forest floor is covered by a soft, spongy duff that grows few plants, and those that do take root are too few for escape cover and not of the right type for food. In forestry jargon, this is a "climax" stand of timber.

Then a fire sweeps the area. A beautiful forest is destroyed—and is reborn.

The ash acts as fertilizer, and the heat of the fire causes the release and germination of seeds. More important, however, the absence of the umbrella branches of tall timber allows sunlight to reach the soil.

For several years, perhaps, the fire area looks black and wasted, but gradually it turns green. And the plant life growing there isn't just one type of tree; it is a cross section of every shrub, grass, weed, and tree native to that region. And in that potpourri of greenery, there is excellent food for wildlife, particularly in the form of winter browse.

Because all the brush is low, the total area gets plenty of sunlight and the entire range experiences a kind of plant explosion. If there is suitable escape cover nearby, it is this kind of situation that is perfect for supporting large populations of deer, not to mention other species of wildlife: grouse, wild turkey, and elk.

Deer Hunting

Under proper management, large numbers of these animals can be harvested each year. In other words, the area begins to develop a reputation as "the best deer hunting in the state." Then, ten or fifteen years later, the number of deer begins to decline.

Overharvest? Poor management? The time to change the season to "bucks only"? Most emphatically no. The forest is changing, and beginning to limit the number of deer it will support.

For the most part, deer food amounts to low-growing brush. If this vegetation grows tall, deer simply can't reach it. Another factor is that when the fire-rejuvenated forest began to grow, the browse went wild. It is the nature of this stuff to take over first.

But under those branches of bitterbrush, chokecherry, or greenbrier, trees were taking root: lodgepole pine, oak, maple, or slash pine—whatever species may be native to the region. Gradually, as they grow taller than the surrounding brush, their leaves and needles shade out the sunlight and the production of deer-supporting vegetation becomes curtailed. As their food source declines, so will the deer, and if the tall vegetation is allowed to grow unchecked, the deer population will continue to slide until it reaches the rock bottom of a climax stage forest, or the forest is again rejuvenated by fire or man.

This was one of the big factors contributing to the decline of Minnesota's deer herd. There, aspen, or "popple" as it is locally called, is a major winter browse. In 1969, 70 percent of the state's aspen groves were thirty years old or older—mature trees with branches far from the reach of feeding deer. In addition, those old, out-of-reach trees were creating shade and thus preventing the growth of young browse plants.

Close to an identical situation occurred in Michigan. In the twenties and thirties northern Michigan was logged heavily. Tall, mature trees were removed and the soil was exposed to sunlight. A deer boom resulted, but now the seedlings of the thirties are approaching maturity and restricting the growth of browse.

Predictably enough, deer populations there are in a corresponding slump.

This "natural" boom-or-bust problem can be, and often is, rectified by man through habitat management. Controlled burns are one tool used. When either the climax species or understory (low-growing plants that take root under the branches of taller trees) isn't of value as timber or food for wildlife, fire, applied judiciously, results in renewed growth and a better-balanced forest. Controlled burns are very common in the South and are catching on in the North. For example, Yellowstone Park administrators have suddenly awakened to the fact that years of fire suppression have changed the balance of their forests—and of the wildlife that lives there. Their policy now is to allow nature-caused fires to burn up 1,000 acres at a time, hopefully bringing 10 percent of their forests back into the regenerative stage.

When mature, tall timber has a market value, a very agreeable arrangement can be struck whereby man harvests the timber and the results of his labors are improved deer habitat. This situation isn't realized, however, by turning an army of loggers with chain saws loose in the woods without direction. Timber must be carefully harvested in small patches to provide maximum "edge" areas (the "edge" where forest meets field is the most productive of browse plants), and some stands of timber must remain unmolested to provide escape cover.

Where selective cutting isn't practical, clear-cutting will produce favorable results, but a representative cross section of plant life must be established in the cleared areas.

In years past, it was common practice to manage a forest for one-of-a-kind growth, encouraging only that species of timber that produced the most profit. It was good business for lumber companies and loggers, but bad wildlife management, so now "islands" of native brush are left to grow undisturbed and reseed themselves (a common technique in the slash pine forests of the South), or wildlife food is encouraged and managed right

Joel Arrington, North Carolina Wildlife Resources Commission

The creation of "edge" areas by selective cutting of mature timber is one way to encourage maximum deer populations.

along with the cash crop (this approach occurs most often in the North and Northwest).

Returning to Deer Island, there is one other aspect of habitat management in current use: direct regeneration. Severely cropped browse plants will never again exhibit the kind of vigor and maximum seasonal growth that might be expected of normal, healthy plants. Replanting selected seedlings, then giving both old and new plants a chance to get ahead of any feeding pressure, is another way to create optimum deer range. But during the period of initial growth, deer must be prevented from cropping the plants.

To achieve this end, many schemes have been attempted— fenced-off sections of range, winter feeding programs, noise and odor devices designed to drive deer away—but only one technique has proved effective and economically feasible: first, direct reduction of herd numbers through hunting; then, permitting a gradual increase in deer numbers with the growth of browse.

The Measurements of Management

Counting the number of deer on a range, then examining the available food source, tells a biologist a lot about carrying capacity. But in sections of the country where cover is dense, the shy nature of deer makes a 1-2-3 approach expensive, time consuming, and very possibly inaccurate.

Besides, knowing the amount of deer within a square mile and the amount of food they have doesn't indicate anything about future herd trends—whether the population is growing, stabilized, or on the decline, or if it is in good, mediocre, or poor health.

Consequently, some sophisticated, scientific yardsticks have been developed to fully determine the condition of deer herds and their future.

Sportsmen provide the subjects for study in the form of the

deer they harvest. From these carcasses, information is gleaned on which management recommendations (next year's seasons, limits, and laws) are based.

Aging by Teeth

"What in the hell are those guys doing, swarming over my deer like that? And poking that thing in his mouth?"

It's a question asked by virtually every sportsman who has ever stopped at a checking station, and I surely admire the checkers' infinite patience, for they are willing to answer the same question over and over again. And they even manage to smile.

It is a common fallacy that you can tell a deer's age by the number of points on his rack. You can't. Age can be determined by a number of involved, sophisticated, laboratory-level tests, and by a simpler and more immediate method initially devised by C. W. "Bill" Severinghaus of the New York Conservation Department: examining a deer's teeth.

Note, I said "simpler." Being able to do this accurately requires both quite a bit of experience and a "jaw board"— examples of jaws from different-aged animals, harvested from the immediate region being surveyed and mounted on a board for comparison.

The technique concerns itself with two areas of examination: tooth replacement and tooth wear. The only teeth examined are the molars in the rear of a deer's jaw. The front teeth, incisors, are unreliable indicators of age.

In their first full year of life, fawns have temporary teeth called "milk teeth," just as a child has baby teeth. If a deer has these teeth, it was born the year of inspection.

When a deer grows to one and a half years old, his first three rear teeth will be worn milk teeth, and the last three sharp, new permanent molars.

At two and a half, the worn milk teeth in the front will have been replaced by new, sharp molars, and the molars in the rear will just begin to show signs of wear.

At three and a half, the first three molars will still be relatively sharp, and the last three will show pronounced wear with brownish lines of dentine exposure woven throughout the enamel. However, at this age and beyond, accurate determination becomes more difficult and requires the eye of a technician with training, since it is totally based on enamel wear.

In most cases you won't have to know how to identify an older animal anyway. Aging by teeth indicates that three and a half year old deer and their elders make up a tiny portion of the yearly take. In Pennsylvania, for example, these older animals average less than 12 percent of the bucks and 25 percent of the does taken annually.

Age composition of the herd is the profile revealed by tooth aging. After a sufficient sample of animals has been examined, it can be determined that the herd in a particular area contains so many fawns, so many one and a half year olds, and so forth. Reduced to percentages, these figures, in turn, reveal population trends for the future.

The technique is based on the knowledge that in a stable herd individual age groups make up a predictable percentage of the total population. The fawn group will always be the largest, accounting for 30 to 40 percent of the deer inhabiting an area. One and a half year olds will make up a smaller percentage, two and a half year olds smaller yet, and so on.

Assuming that antlerless deer hunting is allowed, comparison of the harvest to established herd profiles then reveals population trends.

For example, since the percentage of fawns to adults in a normal herd is a preestablished figure, the antlerless kill should reflect that composition. Fawns should account for the biggest bag. When the number of fawns killed falls far below what is "normal," it is a strong indication that the herd is on the decline—that there aren't enough younger deer to replace those adults which will be removed from the herd by hunting or natural causes.

Conversely, when there are far more fawns than normal, the herd is probably growing. This large fawn crop will become long yearlings the following year, bearing still more young, and exponentially increasing the herd.

These same trends can be revealed during a bucks-only season. Bucks normally grow horns or spikes during their second year, so the lion's share of a buck take should be in this age group. Two and a half year olds, since many were removed from the herd the year before, should make up a smaller percentage, etc.

Determining the age of deer from a jaw board:

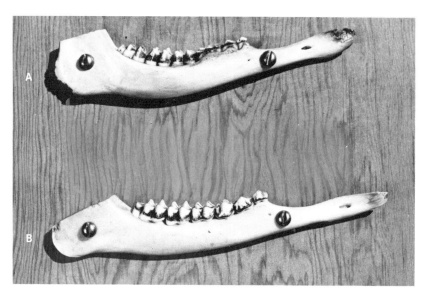

A. 1½ years old—AGE CLASS 1
The three milk premolars are still present and are somewhat worn. The third premolar has three cusps rather than two. The three molars have sharp, pointed crests.

B. 2½ years old—AGE CLASS 2
The three milk premolars have been replaced with three permanent premolars, and these are all sharp, with the enamel about as wide as the dentine. The third premolar has two cusps instead of three; sometimes it looks like only one cusp because the first one is larger than the second.

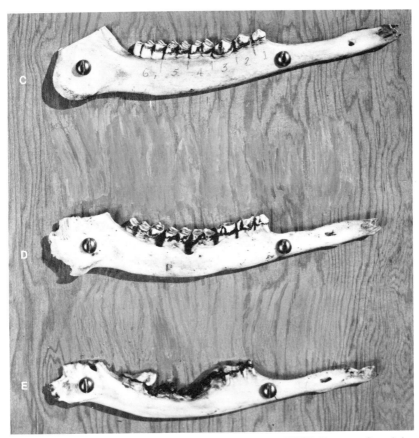

C. 3½ or 4½ years old—AGE CLASS 3

The crests are still fairly sharp-pointed, but the dentine is now wider than the enamel on the third premolar and most of the molars.

D. 5½ to 7½ years old—AGE CLASS 4

The first and second premolars are worn down so that the dentine is wider than the enamel; the crests are worn down level on the cheek side.

E. 8½ years and older—AGE CLASS 5

The molars are worn down to less than one tenth of an inch of the gum line; in some cases they are worn down into the gum, or some of the teeth may have fallen out. The middle part of the molars is worn down so far that there is no longer any trace of the infundibulum. If only the first molar is worn down to the infundibulum, the deer is 7½ years old and belongs in age class 4.

While age composition is a reliable indicator of herd trends, these findings by themselves are neither good nor bad. The statistics have to be balanced with other information such as the condition of the food supply, the general health of the animals, and doe fertility.

Animal Weighing

Chances are that your animal will be weighed as well as being checked for age. This provides one of the many statistics that will be correlated with age distribution of the herd. As with all these other figures, the weight by itself means little. But through past surveys, average weights for healthy animals in each age group have been established. If average weights of this year's harvest compare favorably with those of other years, it is generally a good sign. When the deer taken in a particular year run consistently below an established average, it could point to a deteriorating food source and herd.

Animal Fertility

During antlerless deer seasons, hunters are encouraged to either check in their female animals whole, letting the fish and game people do the job of gutting, or pack back the deer's uterus. The object of this request is to determine the number of young the deer would have borne the next year, if, in fact, she was pregnant at all.

Nature has some unusual ways of handling problems of overpopulation. Along with starvation and disease, it has been found that females in poor physical condition exhibit a low level of fertility. The number of available bucks has nothing to do with the phenomenon. Large groups of does with only one buck have been restocked in areas lacking deer, and tremendous fertility has resulted—three fawns in some does. Conversely, in large, protected populations of deer where the buck percentage was way up, low or no fertility was observed when range and herd conditions were poor.

Antler Development

The size of a buck's antlers means a great deal to the sportsman. It means a lot to the game biologist too, for it is another indicator of the status of a herd.

Let us look first at antler development—how they grow and what they are.

In mid-America, bucks begin to grow antlers in the month of April. The growth is triggered by an increase in male hormones, which in turn is triggered by light—longer days.

The antlers grow from a knob on a buck's head called a pedicel. They grow quite fast, as much as half an inch a day.

During the growing period, they are alive. Flowing blood vessels inside the antler carry the material needed for growth. The blood is kept from escaping by a layer of skinlike material sportsmen call velvet. Indications are that the antlers are quite sensitive at this time; bucks are careful to treat them with kid—buckskin?—gloves, avoiding collisions with brush and trees.

Antlers are usually visible "spikes" by May. The first fork appears in June, and by early August development is complete.

Mid-August finds the antlers hardening. The blood that fed them stops flowing and calcification takes place, beginning at the antler base.

By September, the antlers are no longer "alive." They are impregnated with calcium, and the velvet dries and dies. It is soon removed as the deer rubs against trees and shrubs.

The antlers are carried and polished throughout the rutting season. January is the usual time of loss, because the blood vessels at the very base of the antler constrict then, resulting in a granulation of tissue within the base of the antler pedicel.

It's a little like a foundation crumbling: the antler no longer has a solid connection and is knocked or kicked free or drops off.

Any antler goes through the same process, whether it is a spike or some magnificent, gnarled Christmas tree. So what, then, determines size?

Age, heredity, and locale influence horn growth to a small extent, but the primary factor is nutrition.

• Age: A one and a half year old buck, because his body is still growing, won't exhibit horns as large as those of an older buck. His body is using much of the nutrition that could conceivably go to horn development. One and a half year olds can have four to six points in total, but the antler won't be so big in diameter, height, and width as in an older animal.

• Heredity: Horn size is thought to be an inherited characteristic. If a buck has huge antlers, chances are that his offspring will also carry big racks.

• Locale: This is best explained by an intriguing theory known as "Bergmann's Rule." It holds that in warm-blooded species, larger representatives will always occur in Northern climates, because the larger an animal is, the lower the ratio of his exposed hide area to the elements. Like the high school chemistry sugar-cube experiment, where small cubes dissolve faster than large ones because small cubes have a greater ratio of surface area to bulk, animals with big frames experience less heat loss than those with small frames.

At least in terms of deer, relative weights from different sections of the country support Bergmann. Southern deer are generally small, and Northern deer large. It naturally follows that the bigger the buck's stature, the bigger his rack will be.

• Nutrition is, however, the all-important factor. A Northern deer three and a half years old, with a family tree as impressive as the rack he should carry, will have spindly horns unless he has sufficient food. Horns develop at a time when food and general body condition are at their lowest ebb—in the spring—and the calcium needs of bones and body will be supplied *before* the needs of antlers.

This is especially important in terms of the major age group of bucks, the one and a half year olds. If they are getting enough food, each buck in this range will carry four to six total points.

Georgia Department of Natural Resources

When balanced with other information gleaned from the carcasses of harvested deer, weight reveals herd conditions and trends that in turn will influence future management policy.

If their diet is severely limited, they will be "baldies"—they will carry no rack at all because their bodies used up all the available nutrition developing muscle and bones as they grew into the full maturity of their second year.

Bone marrow is seldom considered as a measurement during regular seasons, since deer are just ending their period of maximum food-availability. It does, however, deserve mention here, since its depth of color is a ready indicator of death by starvation, and consequently an important sign of the need for remedial action.

57

Healthy bone marrow will be white. As a deer begins to go downhill nutritionally, the marrow takes on a pinkish cast, until death by starvation finds it at a stage of color ranging from a deeper pink than the inside of a human mouth to nearly blood-red. The femur, or upper leg bone, contains the marrow most often inspected.

Putting It All Together

Deer management is a science, and in any area of technical study there is always the danger of oversimplification. That is a personal apology to a biologist friend of mine. But in the interest of seeing how all this information influences management recommendations, let us examine some possible profiles collected during an either-sex season from different parts of a state and see what they might mean.

AGE GROUP: 40 percent fawns, 25 percent 1½ year olds. Adults: does and bucks, evenly distributed by age.

WEIGHT: Normal in all groups.

HORNS: Normal. 1½ year old bucks average four total points.

FERTILITY: High. Average 1.5 per doe. This would be the profile of a healthy, stable herd. Management policies in this area are working and should be maintained.

AGE GROUP: 50 percent fawns, 30 percent 1½ year olds. Adult does in excess of normal. Adult bucks decline percentage-wise as a component of herd, 1½ year old bucks increase as a portion of the bag. Indications are that a herd explosion is in the future unless a large harvest of antlerless deer is taken the following year.

AGE GROUP: 50 percent fawns, 20 percent 1½ year olds. Adults still out of balance with the rest of the herd. Few mature bucks, does in excess.

WEIGHT: Down by 10 percent on the average.

HORNS: 1½ year old bucks average spike. Many sublegal bucks observed. A general decline in beam and height measurement in all age classes of bucks.

Deer Management

FERTILITY: 1.2 average per doe. This herd is on the decline. Many 1½ year olds have disappeared, probably killed by winter. Deer-range surveys would indicate a rapid deterioration of food supply. All statistics point to a massive harvest of fawns and does to bring the herd back into balance.

AGE GROUP: 40 percent fawns, 20 percent 1½ year olds. Older does in excess, few adult bucks.

WEIGHT: Down 15 percent from the average.

HORNS: 1½ year old males average sublegal bucks. Many baldies observed.

FERTILITY: .95. This herd is close to rock bottom. Winterkill of yearlings is probably staggering. Fertility has dropped markedly, and the quality of the food source is dismal. A large harvest of antlerless animals is needed badly. The herd must be cut back to half its original size and maintained at that level until the food source improves. The browse must make a comeback before the deer can.

Winter Feeding Pro and Con

Obviously, cold weather is the critical factor in the size and

These three "long-yearling" skulls and antlers well illustrate the effects of good and bad nutrition.

John Hall, Vermont Fish & Game Dept.

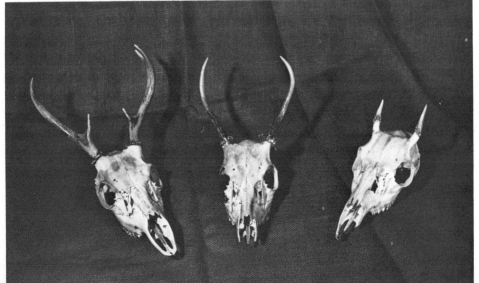

vigor of any deer herd. So why not feed them over the winter? It is a question asked year after year. Aside from hunting itself, no aspect of deer management creates more emotion or controversy.

Why, the public asks, when deer are starving in their Eastern yards and along the great river bottoms of the West, can't they be fed supplemental foods to see them over the critical period?

The question is loaded in its simplicity. First, let us take a look at a typical situation—the kind that occurs year after year in too many states.

It is midwinter. The snow is deep, and deer are dying of starvation. It wouldn't take much money or effort to distribute several tons of hay along the roadside, and, indeed, this is what many individuals have done in the past. What, then, is the effect of their efforts?

Most important, they haven't "fed" the deer. Deer are ruminants, with two stomachs like a cow. Their food is digested and converted into energy by bacteria, but different kinds of bacteria are needed to digest different kinds of food.

Under natural conditions—the relatively slow progress of winter to spring, spring to summer, etc.—the right bacteria have a chance to grow and establish themselves in the deer's stomach as the preferred food gradually changes in composition. But in winter, when a deer is grazing on woody browse, a sudden switch to hay finds him (or his system) unprepared to convert this new food into usable energy. Remember, too, that, except in spring, grasses make up a tiny portion of a deer's diet.

But there is plenty of hay available, with maybe some sweet clover. It tastes good, and there is lots of it. So deer tank up on this readily available food, ignore the hard-to-get stuff that they should be eating, and die of starvation with a full belly and one magnificent last belch of thanks for all that food.

But a number of dead deer isn't the only damage done. Winter feeding obviously concentrates animals. As a matter of fact, I think the "sympathy" and "concern" extended to winter wild-life by feeding programs is more than a little selfish. People enjoy seeing deer, and it's an easy way to achieve this end. It is also an easy way to destroy natural habitat.

The mere effect of thousands of hacking hooves is irrepara-ble damage to whatever browse may be left. There is bound to be some feeding on that browse too. It is cut back even further, and will be able to carry even fewer animals in the future.

Another factor is that deer don't possess either emotions or a value system. They can't conceive of things like pity, or sharing, or kindness. They are animals, and a doe will fill up on food in direct competition with her fawn, often chasing the fawn away from the food. The same is true of a big buck versus a small buck. But those weaker, smaller deer have been lured away from natural available food. They are prime prospects for starvation, thanks to winter feeding.

Just for the sake of argument, however, let us say that winter feeding has been applied judiciously, with minimum damage to the habitat and maximum effort to spread out concentrations of deer, and that somehow the animals have adapted to this new food source. You manage to save the lives of quite a few deer: does carrying fawns, yearlings, bucks. . . .

What are you going to do with all those extra deer, and their offspring, next winter?

Now, an about-face. Deer-feeding programs will work, and are advisable when two criteria are met:

(1). Weather conditions must be unusual and extremely severe.

(2). A means to exclude excess deer created by winter feeding must be incorporated into the next season's harvest.

Let us take a look at precisely what is meant by both these criteria. Severe weather means unusual weather—unusual condi-tions. When snow depth and temperature are considered normal for the area and season, a significant die-off indicates too large

Conventional deer-feeding programs are popular with the public and the deer.

a herd for the range. The solution is a larger kill the next year, not creating more deer.

However, let us say that three feet of snow fall. Then this heavy snowstorm is followed by light rain that thinly crusts the snow surface. Then more snow, and bitter cold. And that cold lasts.

Deer can't move with their normal freedom. Walking, breaking through the crust, not only takes phenomenal energy, but cuts legs like a knife blade as the deer move forward or paw down through the snow.

But the benefits of feeding programs to the public and the deer are debatable.

The animals are extremely limited in that they can't reach a food supply. It is not a problem of unavailable food and overgrazed range. The animals simply are unable to get to the existing ample supply.

This situation justifies feeding attempts, but not those commonly thought of. Rather than luring deer within easy reach of man, humans have to go to them; they have to reach the natural yards by ski, snowshoe, snowmobile, weasel, or whatever, and then supply the animals with natural feed. This is most often accomplished by cutting mature, suitable food vegetation that has grown out of the reach of the animals.

Realize, again, that this is a temporary expedient—an emergency solution. No forest could sustain that kind of cutting winter after winter. It is a measure used only to compensate for a unique condition, and consequently seldom employed.

Note, too, that second criterion. If this unusual measure results in a larger deer herd than is normal, the excess animals must be cropped the following fall. If they are not, overbrowsing and/or excessive winterkill are sure to result during the following winter.

Winter Feeding—A Look at the Future

Conventional and current attempts at winter feeding simply create more problems than they solve. However, the fact does remain that availability of winter food is the determining factor in herd size. Theoretically, if a feasible program of winter feeding of deer were devised, herds could be increased markedly, since summer foods are usually underutilized.

At present, Cornell University is working on a substance that will help deer convert man-grown foods such as hay and grain into digestible material without the normal bacterial transition period.

I have a friend who swears that his deer club in Michigan has a successful winter-feeding program on their leased land, and enjoy more deer because of it. *But* they feed the deer high-grade foods all winter long, not just at critical periods. The cost is, of course, high. Bob figures that his annual buck runs him about $10 a pound!

The prospects of a successful winter-feeding program bring two thoughts to mind. First, if it can be done, more deer must be harvested each year or they will outstrip their *summer* range. Face it, deer have to be controlled at some point or we'll have a Malthusian nightmare whereby deer take over the world!

Second, deer management, though sorely needed and greatly appreciated, could conceivably become so sophisticated that great horned bucks and their graceful does become no more than cattle, led to a predetermined slaughter in defiance of Darwin and his theories of natural selection.

I would hate to see that. I could never hunt a deer that isn't inherently "wild."

I guess I'm a damned romantic after all.

2
The Whitetail

SOME OF THE THINGS about Tango's cabin have slipped into the mist of vague memory, including Tango himself. I can remember that he was a heavy man and wore suspenders and long-sleeved underwear, but beyond that I just remember him as a friend of a friend, who once invited a sixteen-year-old boy up to his deer camp.

It was near a town called Windham, New York, and the snow lay deep that late November, pulling the low branches of the hemlock down to where they nearly touched the ground.

I can recall seeing my first beaver pond there, and cutting down a real Christmas tree, and choking on my first taste of fiery, rot-gut whiskey, much to the delight of the older hunters who came nightly to talk in Tango's cabin. But most of all I remember the deer I shot there: my first whitetail.

It wasn't much—a yearling doe I saw sneaking through a tunnel of snow-covered willow by the beaver pond. And my aim was lousy; it took three shots to connect. But no success has ever been so sweet as the taste of that deer, served in the scrapple we ate at Tango's that night.

Still, my respect for the whitetail isn't totally a matter of

Deer Hunting

nostalgia. Since that day, between guns and cameras I have hunted most species of big game in North America, and I personally rate whitetail as this continent's top trophy.

Part of my reasoning lies in availability: the whitetail is present in every one of the contiguous forty-eight states as well as in Canada and Mexico. This means that they are a quarry available to all comers without limiting factors of long, expensive trips and out-of-state licenses.

Secondly, whitetail are extremely difficult to hunt. Their daily habits just don't lend themselves to easy hunting or beginner's luck. Species such as mountain goat, mule deer, antelope, and elk prefer wide-open spaces where they are relatively easy to find, but whitetail stick to the safety of thick brush where they are tough to see and nearly impossible to stalk. They are also shy animals, bounding off on a zig-zag course at the slightest hint of man: sound, smell, or the flicker of movement.

These two factors make the man who regularly bags a whitetail a special hunter indeed, and the horns, hide, and meat of his animal a real trophy in every sense of the word.

The Whitetail: Description

Two prominent features—tail and horns—immediately identify the whitetail anywhere.

The tail is the most common giveaway: it is large (12 to 18 inches long) and quite bushy. At rest, the topside is brown with a border of white, but woodland walkers seldom see this shade. The most common glimpse they get is the tail's brilliant-white underside, dancing through the woods and disappearing fast.

When whitetail sense the slightest hint of danger, their initial reaction is to raise their tails high in the air, then run like the wind away from the source of their worry. As they do, that brilliant white stands out like a retreating beacon against the dark backdrop of gray woods.

Hunters call this "flagging," and indeed the spot of white,

weaving from side to side in a graceful, bobbing arc, looks very much like someone waving a flag.

Horns on a normal, mature whitetail gracefully curve forward over his forehead and brows. Most definitive, individual points jut upward from a single main antler called the beam. There should be no forking, no perfect "Y" branching of horns on a typical whitetail rack.

There are other less obvious indicators. The ears on a whitetail are proportionately much smaller than those on a mule deer, the only other kind of deer with which a whitetail could be confused. They are roughly the same distance from base to tip as the distance from the ear base to the middle of the animal's head. A whitetail's metatarsal glands are smaller too. These glands are small, smelly strips of hair on the inside of the hind legs, just below the hock. On a whitetail, they are seldom more than an inch long.

The overall body conformation of a whitetail tends to be lean and graceful rather than chunky or massive. Its structure is suited to a 100-yard dash rather than long-distance running, with its slender legs supporting a streamlined torso that is capable of launching it into fast getaways and sudden bursts of speed.

The color of the whitetail is usually rich red-brown in summer, changing to a dull mouse-brown as it grows its winter coat. Color alone is, however, a poor yardstick for identification; in the South and Southwest, specimens living only a few miles apart exhibit variations in coat shade that range from smoky-brown to pollution-gray.

Size is another area of great variety. In general, whitetail living in more northerly latitudes will be larger than their Southern kin. A bragging-size South Dakota whitetail will weigh in at 150 pounds field-dressed, while in Texas all it takes to elicit admiring compliments is 100 pounds of deer. In any section of the country, however, whitetail will be 25 to 33 percent lighter in weight than comparable ages and sexes of mule deer inhabiting the same range.

Deer Hunting

Whitetail Types

The types of white-tailed deer inhabiting this continent are sometimes a subject of argument and confusion. In fact, there is only one species of whitetail in North America, taxonomically identified as *Odocoileus virginianus.*

Over aeons of evolution, populations of whitetail inhabiting specific regions have developed characteristics unique to their kind. These physical differences amount to such features as relative skull size, the length of the metatarsal glands, and tooth structure. The differences are enough, however, to classify these deer types into subspecies, fully thirty of which inhabit this continent.

It is these subspecies that you often hear mentioned in campfire conversation: Northern whitetail, Florida Keys deer, Texas whitetail, and Coues deer, to name a few.

The Coues deer is probably the only subspecies of interest to the sportsman, and only because this whitetail is scored separately in the Boone and Crockett *Records of North American Big Game.*

Whitetail Distribution

White-tailed deer boast a huge range that includes all but the northernmost regions of the North American continent. Populations exist as far south as the Isthmus of Panama, and extend northward to the fifty-fifth parallel, approximately 600 miles north of the Canadian border.

The only areas of the continent where they don't seem at home are the driest regions of the Great American Desert and the high, mountainous country of the West and Mexico.

There is some indication, however, that someday they will extend their range to include these places. Adaptability is one of the whitetail's most prominent traits, and hunters regularly report seeing these deer in places where they were unheard of a decade ago.

The Whitetail

In my native Montana, for example, whitetail have doubled their range since the 1940s, expanding from what was essentially a river-bottom existence to include residence in the foothills of the mountains.

Whether this is desirable is debatable. Many sportsmen claim that whitetail, either by their mere presence or an aggressive nature, drive mule deer away from an area. To date, however, this claim has not been substantiated by scientific fact.

Life History of the Whitetail

The Northern whitetail usually begins life in May. Although there is much folklore associated with the search of does for a

The most common glimpse you will get of a white-tailed deer is a dancing flash of white, disappearing fast.

Michigan Department of Natural Resources

special "fawning ground," verified observation indicates that does drop their fawns wherever they happen to be when the time for birth arrives.

Under healthy conditions, does delivering for the first time have one offspring. Older does usually drop twins, and triplets are not unusual. When they are born, fawns possess spotted coats, a factor that aids in their camouflage. They also lack the functioning scent glands of adults, further deterring detection by predators. Like most members of the animal kingdom, young deer are able to walk and nurse within hours after birth.

For the first four weeks of their lives fawns exist primarily on their mother's milk. During this time, the mother often wanders off from her young in search of food, leaving them curled up in tall grass, under a downfall, or in the middle of like protective cover. It is this situation that often leads to some woodland stroller's finding an "orphan" fawn and taking it home.

In fact, orphan fawns are rare in the extreme. If the doe dies, the young die soon after. Cases of outright abandonment are unheard of.

By their fifth week, young deer begin to feed on tender grasses and shoots. They gradually shift the bulk of their diet from milk to vegetation over the summer, and by midfall it is rare to find a still-nursing fawn. Their protective spots slowly fade over the summer, their "fawn coats" being gradually replaced by thicker winter hair.

Does and fawns usually remain together throughout the first year, and occasionally into the second year. Consequently, these family units often number five or six animals, with several mature yearling deer in the group, one or more of which could be a young buck. The family frequents the same general area throughout the summer months. Their range is seldom more than a square mile, and they commonly feed and bed together.

Although it is possible for seven- to eight-month-old females to conceive, most of them don't reach sexual maturity until the

The new fawn crop is born in midspring. At that time mother and off-spring are extremely secretive, an apparition magically materializing from the dapple of shade and sunlight, but only for those with a quiet step and sharp, sharp eyes.

second year of their lives. The same is true of males, and it is at this time that they grow their first set of antlers.

Depending on the quality of their food source, these antlers can range in size from mere nubbins to four to six total points. When antler growth is complete, these "long yearling" bucks begin to think of mating, and usually leave the family group to live the typical life of a male.

During the pleasant warmer months, male deer live a solitary, aloof existence. They never show interest in their offspring, and concern themselves with other males and females only during the time of the rut in the fall.

As fall approaches, a hormonal change in their body chemistry alters their behavior from reserved to aroused, and bucks begin to wander more. Where the animal's summer range might have been limited to less than a square mile of woods, he gradually extends that domain to include 3 or 4 square miles of territory, frequently walking its boundaries and leaving notice of his presence in the form of urine and musk-scent, sprinkled over patches of pawed earth.

The pitch of his activity continues to rise until the time of actual mating: early to late November in the Northern United States. During this period, bucks are active in the extreme, seldom resting during the daylight hours.

They sharpen and polish their antlers on hardwoods, and continually wander in search of does and encounters with other males. These "fights" are seldom violent affairs. More often they are just pushing contests, but the total energy expended by a male with mating on his mind is considerable. Weight-loss estimates run as high as twenty-five pounds for a large buck.

Does, on the other hand, seem largely uninterested in the affair. They spurn the attention of males until they seemingly have no other choice, and even then are evasive.

Males will remain with a bred doe for a few days, then search out another mate, possibly breeding as many as a dozen does in a season. If a doe doesn't conceive during her first heat cycle, she will usually go through at least two more before the onset of winter and the yarding period, so conception in a healthy female is close to a sure thing.

Weather conditions in the form of deep snows, rather than any particular time of year, usher in the yarding period. At this time, deer of all sexes and sizes congregate around the protection and food provided by deep swamps and brushy lowlands.

It is not any herding instinct that brings the deer together at this time, but just that the best food and cover and the most comfortable living conditions attract the most deer. Yarding does, however, result in something of a mutually beneficial effort. Large groups of deer digging through snow, bucking drifts, and trampling trails results in less energy expended by individuals, and consequently more efficient use of available foods by the entire population.

The deep snows of winter usher in the yarding period, a time when concentrations of deer result in a mutual feeding effort. The yarding period is, however, the time when deer are most vulnerable to disease, starvation, and predation.

Michigan Department of Natural Resources

Deer Hunting

The end of the yarding period is again triggered by circumstance. As melting snows expose bare slopes and spring grass, the big concentrations of deer begin to disperse, lured away by better and more available food. Bucks spend their solitary summers and does and fawns create their small family groups.

Although whitetail achieve a degree of maturity by the time they see their second fall, they don't reach full maturity until their fourth year. This simply means that there is some slight growth each year until that time.

There is no physiological reason why whitetail can't grow to a ripe old age. Deer in captivity have regularly reached twelve to fifteen years, and one venerable old doe didn't die until just before her twentieth birthday. However, few whitetail in nature actually see ten years of life. The rigors of a wild existence, coupled with the pressure of hunting, eliminate virtually all older animals.

In those rare instances when deer do die of "old age," it's not "age" per se that kills them. As is common throughout the animal kingdom, their teeth cause their demise. The teeth become so worn down that they can no longer properly chew their food, and the deer falls prey to starvation and the infirmities of malnutrition.

The Southern whitetail undergoes a history and basic life processes comparable to those of Northern deer, but their sequence and timing become less predictable as you approach the equator.

The reasons why lie in nature's clockwork. The response of most plants and animals to changes in season in Northern latitudes is largely a matter of light fluctuation, not temperature. As the length of daylight increases in the spring, growth in plants is spurred. When it decreases in the fall, growth is retarded. Bird migrations are similarly controlled by light.

The farther south the latitude, the less dramatic the seasonal fluctuation in daylight. Consequently, deer in Florida respond to this stimulus—or lack of it—by dropping their young anytime from June to August and losing antlers anytime from January to March.

Way down south, in southern Mexico, there is even less predictability associated with the yearly cycle. Bucks may have horns any time of year, and does drop fawns in every month.

The winterkill factor is similarly altered. Obviously, there is no snow to produce an extra physical burden on deer populations, but there is a compensating factor: deer in warmer climates experience a significant die-off in the early fall. It is theorized that this is the combined result of excessive heat, a decline in the nutritive quality of the food source, and the increasing strain of lactation and growth on does and fawns. These are the deer most commonly affected by fall die-off.

Whitetail Habitat

Although whitetail enjoy a vast territorial distribution that runs from the heady pines of Canada to the sultry swamps of Central America, they must have suitable habitat to survive.

First and foremost, that means "edges" for food.

Edges are borders of brushy growth that spring up and around the perimeters of forests. While deer do get food from other sources, it is these edge areas that produce the bulk of their yearly nourishment, mostly in the form of low-growing, leafy vegetation.

Typical whitetail foods grown in association with the edge areas of mid-America would include grasses, forbs, aquatic vegetation, the leaves of certain trees, mushrooms, berries, acorns, greenbrier, trumpet vine, strawberry bush, grape, locust, white and red cedar, sumac, wild rose, blackberry, sourwood, white pine, dogwood, piñon pine, mountain maple, ash, oak, birch, hazel, willow, aspen, and viburnum.

In addition to edges and the food that grows there, whitetail need escape cover. This would include dense forests, thick brush, hilly, wooded country, and, in the case of some swamp-dwelling deer, tall grasses.

Realize, too, that because whitetails are not wanderers by nature, both these conditions have to occur side by side if the environment is going to support large populations of deer.

This is one reason why the vast expanse of a virgin forest makes for poor deer hunting. Although you would think that its sheer isolation would find it crawling with wildlife, there isn't that much suitable food there. The opposite is true of intensively farmed areas, where virtually every acre has felt the bite of a plow. There may be plenty of food available, but there is no escape cover.

On the other hand, dense timber with small but frequent patches of clear-cut makes ideal whitetail habitat. And so do farms and ranches where woodlots are allowed to stand side by side with croplands, fallow fields, and pastures.

Whitetail Habits

A whitetail begins its day before the first pale light of dawn. These deer are often nocturnal feeders, and at least some of their meal is usually taken before light. Feeding periods last between one and three hours, and the morning meal tapers to a close around sunup.

A whitetail's habits classify it as a skulker, a form of behavior that finds this animal preferring to remain in or near the protection of thick brush. Consequently, feeding areas will always be close to some kind of cover.

Seldom will you see whitetail feeding in the middle of an alfalfa field without the safety of darkness. In daylight hours, they will always be strung out along its borders. Even the irresistible lure of an apple orchard will find them first feasting on the fruits that have fallen close to the woods or tall grasses. Natural feeding areas tend to be tiny parks of shrubs and grasses, where dappled sunlight makes them hard to see.

After the feeding period whitetail return to their beds by a route that again takes them through the cover of brush. Beds are

Whitetail are skulkers by nature—creatures of thick brush and dense woods where they easily elude pursuit.

usually quite close to the feeding grounds, seldom more than half a mile away.

Whitetail don't use the same bed every day, though they will use the same general area for bedding for months at a time. The place they choose for their daily bed is largely determined by the weather.

If the weather is hot, look for bedded deer in cool, shady spots. If the weather is cold but sunny, expect them to choose a spot in the sun, probably on a southern exposure if the country is hilly. When it is cold and stormy, look to the tall timber and the roof provided by the tentlike branches of conifers. Should a strong wind be blowing, search out spots where the wind can't reach and where all the sounds associated with wind—creaking trees, snapping branches—are muted. This is most often a deep swamp, a dense stand of timber, or a well-wooded gully.

No matter where the weather directs them, whitetail choose a spot for their actual bed that is surrounded by low, thick cover. On a sunny slope, they lie down in the middle of a stand of wild roses or tall grass. When they are in tall timber, they lie under a tree whose trunk is surrounded by brushy juniper rather than one growing where there is no understory. This, too, is tied to their skulking nature; whitetail rely heavily on sound and smell, rather than sight, to herald the approach of a predator. Then they use their bedding cover as a blind to slip away unseen.

The part water plays in a whitetail's day is debatable. They occasionally take a drink after eating, but the need for water isn't the driving, dependable force that their need for food is. They get the bulk of the liquids their body requires from the succulent foods they eat.

Whitetail spend the daylight hours in their bedding area. Occasionally they arise and pensively walk around the immediate area, and around noon they may even nibble on nearby vegetation, but for the most part serious feeding doesn't resume until evening.

This period of movement and activity begins one hour before

sundown and continues beyond the point of total darkness. Deer behavior at this time is identical to that at the morning feeding period: they travel routes that take them through thick brush and feed close to the protection of cover.

This sketch of a whitetail's day remains relatively constant so long as conditions do. There are, however, times when their behavior and response patterns will be altered. One common cause is hunting pressure.

Hunting pressure tends to make whitetail even more secretive. They feed earlier and later to take advantage of darkness, and spend less time eating.

Although the presence of large numbers of hunters in the woods would logically make the deer nervous and skittish, their bedding behavior seems to indicate the opposite reaction. Rather than getting up and bolting off at the first sound of a footfall, whitetail tend to hold an even tighter position than is normal.

A big buck was once fitted with an electronic sending unit at the start of hunting season. Fish and game officials traced his movements with a receiver, and during a three-week period, in a heavily trafficked area, they found that many hunters walked within 10 feet of the animal and never knew he was there. Several noisy drives went right by him, other deer were shot nearby, and still he stayed put in whatever bed he had chosen for the day. He came through the season without a scratch.

Nor does hunting pressure seem to move whitetail out of an area. Indeed, hunters see fewer deer because the animals judiciously avoid exposure. But whatever number of whitetail were around at the beginning of the season will remain within their territory no matter how much pressure occurs, unless, of course, they are killed by hunters.

Weather has a significant effect on whitetail too. Pleasant, sunny, dry weather encourages early and late feeding. Since deer don't use up much energy in this kind of weather, feeding periods will be short.

In rainy, cloudy weather feeding periods occur later and earlier and deer movements are increased. At these times deer are not overly alert, perhaps lulled into complacency by the quiet of the woods and the many strong smells associated with a rain.

Windy, blustery days make deer nervous, probably because of all the creaking and rustling of trees and leaves, and the swirling air currents that can carry smells from indefinable directions. Deer become extremely alert at this time.

Heavy storms of either snow or rain force deer to remain bedded for extended periods. During the storm they hole up in dense cover and sit tight. After the storm passes, they become quite active, filling up their empty stomachs during long feeding periods.

Bitter cold elicits an unusual response in whitetail. When it gets far below zero, they lie down without moving until the weather breaks. It is thought that their instinct is to conserve energy and hold heat loss to a minimum, which is precisely the effect of their self-enforced immobility.

Within the framework of day-to-day living, whitetail exhibit a variety of individual responses that are interesting to the hunter and the naturalist. For the most part, they function to either ferret out possible danger or to warn other deer of its presence.

• Whitetail have a kind of semaphore system involving their tail and rump hairs. When they are calmly feeding, their tails switch much like the tails of cows or horses; up and down, side to side. At the slightest hint of danger, the tails stop moving except for a barely perceptible twitch. When danger is further identified, they raise their tails high. This exposes their white rump hairs and flares them out in a dazzling brightness very different from the shade of their white hairs when laid flat. The white is extremely visible against any sort of background, and it is thought that the sight of it is a silent warning to any other deer in the neighborhood to be on the alert. Once a whitetail's

The tail of a white-tailed deer amounts to a silent semaphore system. When it goes up, danger is thought to be nearby, and the animal can be expected to run soon after.

tail is in the air, he is sure to bound off within seconds.

• Stamping finds a whitetail jumping a few inches off the ground, then coming down with a hard thump. It is usually a trick used when deer aren't sure of some object they see and can't further identify it. Stamping has a startling effect on the subject under scrutiny and is also a form of communication. Deer have sensitive feet, and other deer nearby are put on alert by the vibrations traveling through the ground.

• Blowing is another trick deer use when they are frightened. They flare their nostrils, then suddenly expel a gust of air. The sound is roughly a cross between a sneeze and a bark, and the action is thought to be both a surprise tactic that might frighten a predator into revealing himself and a way to clear mucus from their nostrils for a better sense of smell.

Deer Hunting

It is an effective trick; I defy any unknowing hunter to remain stock-still when a deer blows at close quarters. I regularly clear the ground by 3 feet. Then, too, there is always the urge to blurt out "Gesundheit."

• A deer in doubt will stand perfectly still for long periods of time, but there is one part of his anatomy that will move: his ears. They twitch this way, then that, in a constant search for an identifying sound, and it is this little bit of movement that often reveals their presence to a sharp-eyed observer.

• Whitetail can be counted on to work in a circular pattern when confronted with potential danger, and that circle will usually swing downwind. When a deer spots something he can't identify that piques his interest, he often retreats out of sight, then reapproaches that spot with the wind on his face. Even a thoroughly spooked deer, one that has been jumped by a hunter, will often run straightaway, then circle back downwind to double-check the source of his fright.

• A whitetail's entire being is attuned to identifying and eluding potential enemies on the ground, but he never expects danger from above. Consequently, using platform stands and posting in trees are among the most effective ways to hunt this animal.

Hunting the Whitetail

Savage Arms Corporation once did a study in Michigan. Thirty-nine deer—seven bucks, fourteen does, and eighteen fawns —were fenced in a mile-square area, and experienced hunters were turned loose on the property. The "hunters" only looked; they didn't carry firearms.

Six hunters spent four days before they found their first buck. In the next four weeks, "buck sightings" averaged fifty-one hours' worth of walking in the woods. The shortest time in the woods for the sighting of any deer—buck, doe, or fawn—was fourteen hours.

There are several reasons why these "captive" deer, and whitetail everywhere, are able to regularly outwit hunters. First, they possess an intimate knowledge of every topographical feature in their home range. They know what paths lead to dense cover, which way to turn to get a hill or hedge between you and them, and what stand of brush is too thick for a human to pass. They are also aware of changes that occur in their territory; they will avoid a new-fallen tree for a week or more until they get used to the idea of its being around. Hang a slip of cloth in a bush and a deer will spend an hour watching it, perhaps slowly advancing for a closer inspection a step at a time.

Another thing that effectively baffles hunters is a whitetail's confident reliance on camouflage for protection. Most hunters simply can't conceive that a deer can escape their notice at 10 to 15 feet, but they frequently do.

There is also their skulking nature. Because they favor dense brush and possess extremely keen senses, they are virtually impossible to approach afoot. Even when a hunter opts to put them in a position where they have to come to him—by posting on a deer stand, for instance—human nature works for the whitetail.

Man is neither physically nor mentally attuned to sitting motionless for long periods of time, particularly when there is also the element of discomfort: cold, or the rubbly cushion of hard, stony ground. So he moves. Perhaps he simply adjusts his hat, scratches his head, or stamps his feet to get some circulation going, but a whitetail will pick up that flicker of movement immediately and be off.

The cardinal rule to bagging a whitetail, then, is to know those areas where he is the expert and refrain from challenging him on those grounds. Instead, pick his weaknesses and capitalize on them.

Of those weaknesses, none play into a hunter's hands so well as the failure of the deer to expect danger from above.

Any man who has observed whitetail on the ground knows

that they possess infinite savvy about the world around them and that they are able to correctly react to danger in the span of a heartbeat. I personally had them pegged as one of the smartest animals in the woods until my first encounter with one from 8 feet in the air.

I was perched on the limb of an old, gnarled oak in northern Florida. The forests of northern Florida consist of dense jungles of slash pine, live oak, brier, and Spanish moss, where seeing deer from a post on the ground is almost impossible. My tree stand was indeed the only practical approach.

I had been there for an hour, having climbed up in the light of a red, smoky dawn. The forest was alive with morning sounds: chattering squirrels, chirping cardinals, and the jackhammer tapping of big pileated woodpeckers, but even with all that noise the sudden snap of a twig to my right seemed as clear as a rifle shot. Something was moving in the thicket.

I held my breath, dropped my thumb to my rifle hammer, and watched the brush until my eyes began to burn. Then a deer stepped into plain view, not 30 feet away by line of sight.

It was a doe, and Florida had a buck law, so I eased my thumb off the hammer and watched quietly. The deer seemed to have some notion of my presence; in the span of thirty seconds, she dropped her nose to the ground twice, then swung her head in a wide arc, examining the surrounding brush for some other sign to affirm what her nose indicated.

"P-s-sst," I whispered.

She stiffened, motionless except for the barest quivering of her tail and a constant twitching of her ears. Slowly she lowered her head once more, sniffing. She seemed to be peering under the brush.

"Hey . . . up here!" I called in a low voice.

The animal startled, then stamped her front feet in a little, impulsive jump. She snorted, and dust and leaves swirled on the ground in front of her nostrils. Her tail stiffened, too, like a

This trophy-class whitetail fell prey to the most effective trick in the book: hunting from a tree stand.

Deer Hunting

bird dog on point. Then, with measured, exquisite precision, she took one carefully clocked step forward.

She was plainly tensed to run, but seemed not to want to take off until she could positively identify the nature of the sound and smell. It was either a matter of dogged inquisitiveness or the need to know which path would take her away from potential danger. I tend to favor the latter explanation, since my last clue in our game of hot and cold was to drop my hunting knife 2 feet in front of her nose. As it hit the ground, she leaped like a released clockspring, whirling away from the sudden sound and movement.

But she seemed to be inquisitive too. Rather than bounding away, the typical spooked-whitetail reaction, she strode off like a mule deer, twice glancing back at the spot where the knife had hit—still interested, I assumed, in finding out exactly what had happened.

The incident was interesting in its own right, but what really impressed me about that deer's reaction was her total ignorance of my location. Using all the magnificently developed senses at her disposal, she never once considered looking up, even though I gave her ample opportunity and indication.

Another advantage offered by elevation is visibility. At ground level, your view is always restricted by brush. When you get up high, you can see over understory growth, and to some extent down into it. This makes spotting a deer infinitely easier, and is as helpful in hunting whitetail as the deer's reluctance to look up.

Many hunters who want to watch from an elevated stand assume that a suitable tree will be available wherever they choose to hunt. That is not usually the case. A "natural" tree stand requires a rather old, sturdy tree, with large, low branches for foot- and handholds and a comfortable place to nestle while you wait. There just aren't many trees like that in most woods. What is more, finding one that is close to probable areas of deer activity further complicates the problem, so unless you know that a suitable perch exists in the place you want to hunt, it's better to provide your own. There are two types to consider.

Permanent stands afford the advantage of comfort. Depending on how elaborate a stand you want, these can range in size from small wooden platforms to rather roomy affairs with roof and walls to keep out the weather. Permanent stands can either be built in large trees or on stilts, like the type of chair used by lifeguards.

Unless you have a lease on private ground, permanent stands are first come/first served no matter who built them. Because of this drawback, portable stands are perhaps more practical for the bulk of today's hunters. They can be used anywhere you want to set them up, will lock in place in a matter of minutes, and afford you a seat that is exclusively yours.

You can make these stands in a home workshop or buy them (see page 92). Most of them work on a leverage principle whereby a brace is attached to a tree by a chain and tightener. The brace leads from the securing chain to the outer edge of the platform. The inner edge of the platform rests against the tree trunk, and when a hunter stands or sits on the platform, the inner edge digs firmly into the tree, providing safe support without the use of nails.

These stands do present the problem of getting them up a tree; you are either limited to well-branched trees or you have to carry a ladder.

Another alternative to consider is a climbing tree stand. These ingenious devices actually climb trees with a little help from the hunter.

Their construction and the principle on which they work are roughly the same as the conventional platform, except that a rigid brace of edged metal is substituted for the anchoring chain, and webbed bindings are provided for your feet.

You begin the climbing process by facing the tree with your feet in the bindings. The procedure is a little like shinnying. With arms wrapped around the tree, you draw your feet and the

Climbing tree stands are anchored to a tree trunk by leverage. Webbed bindings fit over your feet.

attached platform up under you. Bear down on your heels and up on your toes, and leverage forces the platform into secure place on the trunk. Stand up straight, get another firm grip with your arms, draw your feet up once again, and you are on your way up.

In place, the design of these platforms is such that they can't slip once there is weight on them. They do present something of a problem, however, in the way your feet are attached to them. It is quite possible for your feet to slip free of their bindings as you draw the platform up, and when this happens, the platform slides down the tree trunk, leaving you stranded at whatever level you happen to be. It is one of deer hunting's more embarrassing moments.

90

The tree is climbed by a process similar to shinnying. The stand is drawn up with your feet.

In place, the climbing tree stand provides a safe, stable, and, most important, portable hunting platform.

Deer Hunting

The best of both the portable and climbing tree stands on the market fold up and have carrying straps so they can be toted on your back like a pack to and from the tree of your choice. One manufacturer is the Baker Manufacturing Company of Valdosta, Georgia.

Since you must wait for the deer to come to you, heavily used game trails are the best places to set up a stand and morning and evening are the best times to hunt. As a rule, 10 feet of elevation will keep a deer from discovering you, though you may well want to go higher for a clearer view.

Safety and common sense dictate extreme caution when you are climbing a tree with firearms. It is best to remove all cartridges from your gun when you plan to climb. The reason for this added precaution is that in climbing it is quite possible for your action to open and close without your being aware of it.

Driving deer is, I feel, the second most effective hunting technique. Walking hunters force the deer to move, and as they try to avoid the stalkers, they will theoretically pass by hidden still-hunters.

It's a productive method of hunting whitetail, particularly in the middle of the day when deer lie up and remain inactive, but there are several conditions that have to be met if you are going to have both a successful and safe hunt.

First, drivers must stay within view of each other. You don't have to see every driver in the line—just the man on your right and the one on your left. That way, whitetail can't pull their circling trick and double back without being seen. From a safety standpoint, this practice also keeps all the drivers moving abreast on an even line. There is no danger of a zigzag line of walkers, and a man blundering into the line of fire. It goes without saying that no driver ever takes a shot sharply to his left or right.

Posters—still-hunters—are safest as well as most successful when they are up high. That way, their shots will be angled downward, and any shots the drivers take will be at ground level. In the event that posters are on the ground, it is important to prearrange a time at which the posters take no more shots in the direction of the drivers or vice versa.

Drives require only half as many posters as walkers, and the technique is most effective when you work out small blocks of terrain at a time. I would rate a quarter of a square mile as the largest area you should ever attempt to drive. When there is dense cover, the area worked over should be much smaller.

The amount of noise necessary for an effective drive is a matter of debate; some nimrods claim that drivers have only to walk naturally to move deer out ahead of them, while others maintain that whistling, yelling, and beating on drums work best. I tend to lean toward the noisy end of the spectrum. It seems to confuse the animals more, and they will approach the posters without so much customary and cussed caution.

Solo standing is probably the most popular form of whitetail hunting, and it involves nothing more than waiting quietly along a well-used game trail.

My reservations about the effectiveness of this technique are all tied in with the hyperactive nature of human beings. It is virtually impossible for anyone short of a meditating guru to remain motionless for long periods of time. And this is the only way to ensure that a deer will wander into range.

But for all its drawbacks, posting is sometimes the best way to hunt. Tree stands are illegal in some states, and in others circumstances may find you in a situation where there are no suitable trees for climbing or where you haven't built or brought your own stand.

Should you wish to post, there are several measures you should take to mask both your presence and potential movement. The first is to build a blind.

One of the more common claims of whitetail hunters that I personally believe to be a myth is the notion that all you have to do to camouflage yourself is to break up your outline by crouching down next to a convenient bush or tree trunk. I find that this claim is faulty on three counts:

First is the simple matter of exposure. Any movement on your part will be plain to see.

Second, whether you move or not, whitetail possess so intimate a knowledge of their home territory that even the static bulk of a hunter sitting far away may well indicate something out of place and put them on the alert.

Third, I believe that wearing bright colors makes a hunter more easily seen by a deer. And yes, I am aware that there are no cones in a deer's eye and that they are not supposed to be able to discern colors. But wearing camouflage during archery and spring gobbler season, I have often had deer hear and wind me, and not see me, at 25 yards. When I wear red, both in and out of season, deer seem to be able to spot me from way off without the use of their other senses.

Perhaps it's a matter of relative light intensity on a gray scale; deer see the brightness of red and orange, not the color. Whatever the explanation, I firmly believe that bright colors work to a hunter's disadvantage. They are certainly necessary for safety, but a blind helps break up their brightness without sacrificing the safety factor.

When building a blind, keep two things in mind: it should fit in perfectly with the surroundings and cover you from all quarters. Construct it in a place and in such a way that you don't alter the original appearance of the area. If you do somehow change the visual environment—say by piling broken limbs from big pine trees against the basic brown of low brush—there is a good chance that whitetail will note the change and avoid the area entirely for several days.

Comfort is another way to increase your odds. The more comfortable you are on a stand, the longer you will be able to remain there and the less you will fidget. Wear warm clothes so that the cold won't tempt you to move around. Bring a sitting pad so that hard ground won't make you change your seat every five minutes.

The final ingredient of successful posting, be it in a tree stand or on the ground, is patience. The man who can sit for long hours is the one who will see deer, and again this quality goes somewhat contrary to human nature: man is an impatient being.

To overcome that impatience, try a little trick I learned from a friend who dabbled in Eastern religion.

"From birth, humans are trained to produce things," he once told me. "Work, thoughts, words, dreams; we always have to be doing something, putting something out. Instead of output, just once become a creature of input. Sit down, clear your mind, and take things in. Sounds, smells, the sight and touch of the world around you."

It's a staggering experience on the deer stand. The sound of a squirrel scratching for nuts takes on monumental importance. The patterns of sunlight dancing through leaves become intriguing beyond description. The tingle of wind on your face and its passage through the branches of trees speak a whole new language, but one you come to understand. It seems a contradiction, but truly hearing all the messages as you sit in a quiet fall woods is an indescribably exciting experience. And in that absorbent state, you will discover that time isn't measured and patience becomes literally and figuratively natural. Then, too, you are so much aware of the world around you that it is quite likely you will notice a deer before he discovers you. It has happened to me so often that "input" is now my reverent attitude whenever I am in the woods.

Still-hunting is the most difficult whitetail hunting technique, for in this situation all the odds are in the deer's favor.

You will improve your chances if you stalk with a partner. This technique, called "walk and wait," requires that one hunter remains still and watchful while the other advances. When the walking hunter is 50 to 60 feet beyond the waiter, the still-hunter becomes the stalker. The spacing between the two hunters is strictly a matter of cover density. Your partner should be in clear sight of you at all times; otherwise you could well fail to see deer he might push out.

Still-hunting alone is tough but, like posting and listening, it's a very personal way to hunt and one I favor just for the pleasure it affords. The cardinal rule is to remember to use your eyes fifty times more than your feet.

When you take your first step into a forest, you are viewing a new world, but what most hunters fail to realize is that every succeeding step reveals still another world.

One step forward changes the relative position of trees. You are seeing a slightly different side of them as well. The change of position also opens up avenues of sight down lanes of brush and between tree trunks, and closes up some of those that were open before.

Use your eyes to judge the placement of your next step. Absolute quiet and slow, deliberate, rather than jerky, body movements are two other keys to walking up on deer.

Because you are truly playing the deer's game, you are far better off to hunt in territory that is familiar to you, rather than in territory you have never hunted before. Knowing the "lay of the land" adds up to some weighty advantages for the hunter.

For example, you will remember from past experiences how to approach a small woodland edge unseen. You will know the trails deer favor without having to scout them out first. And you will remember the trick that big buck pulled on you last year, and perhaps cut him off as he doubles back.

It is extremely important, too, to know what a deer looks like in the woods, and I am not being facetious. Perceiving a deer against the backdrop of a dark forest bordering a field, or through a screen of brush, is far different from viewing one in a zoo or on the pages of a magazine.

Look for outlines first. Generally, nature arranges things in one of two ways: in straight lines (the trunks of trees and the horizon) or in semicircles (a tree's crown of leaves, mountains, and rocks). Look for patterns that don't fit into this scheme, such as the angular conformation of a deer's body.

Movement is another giveaway. A whitetail will stand stock-still until he decides to run, but he will twitch his ears until he makes up his mind. Once you learn what to look for, it is surprisingly easy to spot that twitching.

Color is perhaps the poorest determinant. Under the changeable conditions of natural light, deer can appear to be every shade from black to rust-red. A spot of white, however, does deserve closer examination. Occasionally its presence will magically reveal the outline of a deer attached to it.

Always still-hunt with the wind on your face, and if possible with the sun on your back. That way, you will cut the chances of a deer's smelling and seeing you.

It is extremely important, I feel, that deer—both muley and whitetail—should not be able to wind a walking hunter. And both situation and wind shifts can often put the wind on your back. To counter this possibility, as soon as I find a hunter with a deer, I beg, borrow, or steal the animal's musk glands, and from that point on until the end of the hunting season, I leave one in each pocket of my hunting jacket.

That the trick is effective is undebatable; just leave that jacket in a closed room for a day and the place will smell like a deer farm. I once made the mistake of going on an extended winter vacation right after deer season without removing the glands from my jacket. On our return, it took a week to air out the house, and two weeks to placate my wife. So should you try this trick, you might consider hanging the jacket in a garage during the hunting season and sending it to the cleaners when it is over.

Whether you are still-hunting or standing, shoulder your gun immediately whenever you see a deer. From that posture, you can decide if it has horns or, in fact, if it is a deer. Should you decide to shoot, your aim will then be far more accurate than a shot fired from a gun that was snapped into position at the last split second of decision.

Joe Arata, an old and good friend of mine, is one of the most successful whitetail still-hunters I know—and he regularly scores in the heavily hunted woods scant miles from New York City. The advice he once gave to me involves still another aspect of deer hunting: faith.

"Anytime you're in the woods, you've got to figure there's a whitetail nearby: behind some bush, moving down a trail, or lying at the base of a tree. The trick to hunting them isn't to cover a lot of ground; it's just to see them before they see you.

"Once you can train yourself to believe deer are nearby, and learn to do a lot of quiet looking in the right places, you'll be amazed at just how many whitetail will really turn up in your immediate neighborhood."

Calling deer is a technique frequently used with whitetail, and it is most often done in conjunction with some sort of blind or tree stand. Deer calling works best during the rutting period, since the object is to attract a male within range either by the bleat of a doe, or by the rattle of horns to simulate a battle.

Deer calls imitate the doe. A deer call is usually a cedar or plastic box over which is stretched a rubber band. When blown, the rubber band vibrates, producing a sound that falls somewhere between the blat of a sheep and the hoarse yelp of a dying rabbit.

The best device for rattling up a buck is a pair of old antlers. These are merely clicked and clacked together, as they might be when two bucks square off.

Both types of calls will draw deer near, but there is a temptation on the part of the hunter to overuse them. Doe don't walk around the woods bleating every five minutes, and even though bucks may fight a pitched battle for an hour or more, if a hunter does nothing but rattle horns all day chances are that either his movements will give him away or he will simply fail to detect an approaching deer.

Remember that a little bit of calling goes a long way. For best results use your call sparingly—or not at all.

Floating is a technique that is quite effective and generally overlooked. Since whitetail and their sharp senses seem to be lulled by the sound of water, a good way to spot a deer is to launch a canoe or jonboat in a sluggish stream and float silently along, watching the shore.

In large rivers, floating also provides silent access to islands that often boast huge populations of whitetail. In eastern Montana, my friends and I often hunt islands in the Yellowstone River by floating. We use two boats, with three hunters in each, and drop four of the hunters off on the upstream end of the island. The two boatmen then drift to the downstream end of the island, beach their craft, and take up a stand. At a prearranged time, the drivers start pushing through the brush. The technique seldom fails to produce action.

The same concept that makes floating effective can also be extended to wading and stalking down a tiny brook.

Dogging deer is a popular sport in the South. There the woods are so dense that a significant harvest of whitetail would be impossible without some canine assistance. But there is a lot more to whitetail, Southern style, than a few dogs and a hunter.

Linguists have traced the roots of the Southern drawl back to England, and I think their thesis holds up in terms of hunting too. In the British Isles, anything to do with dogs and hunting comes attached to the pleasant formalities of ritual and tradition, and that is just the case on a Southern deer hunt.

Tradition hangs as thick as a humid night over the ramshackle deer camps of the South and in the bloodlines of sleek hounds, both of which are handed down from father to son.

The night before the hunt is the time to sip bourbon, argue dogs, and spin yarns of the past.

Deer Hunting

The twilight of the next morning is when you eat the ritual meal: country-cured ham, eggs, and grits (if you don't know what that creamy, granulated stuff is, don't ask!)

The hunt begins when shooters are posted at strategic locations: along game trails, firebreaks, logging roads, and railroad tracks. Then the anxious, whining hounds are turned loose: redbones, blueticks, and black-and-tans.

At first you hear a few pensive yips, and maybe a hurried dogfight on the run. Then suddenly the pack strikes a hot trail and breaks into a cacophony of bawls and yelps that fill the silent woods like the gong of a great bell.

"That's old Rattler at the head of the pack," you will hear a proud owner boast to anyone within earshot.

Suddenly the frenzy of the pack raises a pitch. They have jumped a deer. True to its instinct, the whitetail doesn't run out of the country, but keeps circling back, milling around, staying within the territory he knows so well. Sometimes he runs past a hunter on stand and a gun booms out. Sometimes the deer thoroughly eludes the dogs and they run more quietly until they strike a new trail. Sometimes that pack of baying, singing hounds heads in your direction, and at that time I defy anyone to maintain a normal heartbeat.

Dogging is definitely an exciting way to hunt deer.

Youngsters have a part in this tradition too. Similar to the European practice of the jaeger's presenting an oak leaf stained with blood to the man who shot the biggest stag, Southern boys who shoot their first buck are "blooded" with a slash of deer blood placed on their foreheads by their father or the head of the hunt. Kids have been known to go for a week without washing their faces after receiving this badge.

One other piece of Southern tradition deserves mention in connection with a deer hunt. When you miss a shot at a buck, you lose your shirttail. The bigger the buck, the bigger the chunk that is taken. The tail is then hung up back at camp, and the offending hunter is required to wear his mutilated shirt until he makes appropriate amends, ranging from supplying camp with a bottle of good bourbon to shooting an even bigger buck.

The shirttail, however, remains in camp, and it's not uncommon to see forty or fifty of the slips of cloth hanging on a wall. It helps ease the pain a little to know that so many other hunters missed. And I speak with the voice of experience; I once left a rather substantial hunk of red flannel on the wall of a cabin in the Georgia piney woods.

Montana Department of Fish and Game

3
Mule Deer

THEY SAY THAT first impressions are a poor measurement of character, and in terms of people I agree. But mule deer . . . well, that's a different matter.

I saw my first muley in 1959, the year I moved to Montana. I had left New York two days earlier to clatter across America by train. The North Coast Limited had left Minneapolis the evening before; after bellowing through North Dakota during the night, it crossed into Montana in the dark of predawn. Eager to get my first look at the wide open spaces, I arose at first light and, without so much as a cup of coffee to pry open my drooping eyelids, groped my way up to the dome car to stand in respectful awe of the vista that greeted me.

To my right ran the Yellowstone River, milky with the silt of the prairie. Its waters wound around islands of cottonwoods and willows, crowned with fall yellows and browns. Beyond the river stretched a mighty sweep of dry, grassy plains that dished up to form the crests of bare, brooding hills.

Ahead, far in the west, stretched a smoky-blue outline of sawtooth magnificence, capped by a glimmer of white—the Rocky Mountains.

There were no neat squares of fenced fields for perspective, no comfortable red barns for shelter. The land was vast, a challenge to the eye and impossible to digest all at once, but it was wild and it was beautiful.

The track ran close to a low cliff on my left, cut into the bedrock by the waters of the river long ago. The observation deck was nearly level with the top of the rock wall, and I could see that it sloped up into rolling domes of shaly soil that were dappled with powder-blue sage. Then I saw that mule deer. He was skylighted on one of the domes, and all muscle compared to the dainty whitetail I had known: squarish, massive, and gray as the rock on which he stood. Beneath him grazed two does.

He paid the passing train no heed until the engineer acknowledged his presence by two long whistle blasts. Even then, he only raised his head for the briefest look, and in doing so revealed a magnificent set of antlers that spread like a bush, out and up beyond the width of his great shoulders. Then he returned to his meal.

It wasn't an incident of earthshaking magnitude—just my first look at a muley. But I still remember the moment, for there was something in his surroundings, his appearance, and his regal gesture that defined the species in the span of a few seconds. A unique casualness, subdued strength, and raw beauty—that was my vision of the muley then. Fourteen years' worth of trails, tracking snow, and spent cartridges later, that view hasn't changed a bit.

Mule Deer: Description

The mule deer (*Odocoileus hemionus*) is a large animal. Prime Northern males often reach 300 pounds live weight. They attain a shoulder height of 42 inches and a body length of up to 6 feet.

As a species, the mule deer's most prominent feature is their ears. They are enormous and mulelike, and extend out from the side of the head when they are investigating a sound.

A mule deer's tail is short—only 6 to 8 inches long—and has a

Enormous ears, a cream-white rump and small, black-tipped tail, and horns that fork or "Y" immediately identify the mule deer.

prominent black tip. When alarmed, a mule deer carries its tail at rest or perpendicular, but never erect. Viewed from the rear, a mule deer's rump appears to be almost entirely cream or buff-white in color, except for its black-tipped tail.

Antlers on a mule deer buck "Y" or fork, then fork again in symmetry, instead of branching off one main beam. Antlers spread in a U-shape out over the ears, rather than curving over the forehead. On both sexes of mule deer, the metatarsal gland is 2 or more inches long and is surrounded by black hair.

Like other members of the deer family (Cervidae), muleys shed their coats in the spring and fall. Their coats will bleach out when exposed to the sun for long periods of time, and consequently their color runs from gunpowder gray in the fall and winter to reddish brown in the late spring and summer.

The makeup of a mule deer's coat reflects the heritage and environment of these animals. The outer layer of hair—guard hair—is coarse, thick in diameter, and stiff. Underneath the guard hair is a layer of fine fur, soft, fluffy, and gray as goose down. Laid flat, this coat makes for a thin, cool covering in hot summer. Bristled out, it traps enough dead air to keep the animal alive during the bitter minus forty degree weather that sweeps down from the Arctic every Western winter.

Mule Deer Types

Like the whitetail, mule deer from various regions have developed into subspecies of mule deer within their present range of distribution.

There are two subspecies that deserve special mention. The Columbian black-tailed deer and the Sitka deer are two closely allied types that inhabit the rain forests of the Pacific coast from northern California to lower Alaska. Like the Coues whitetail, they are scored separately by Boone and Crockett, but they are also considered by some to be a separate and distinct species from mule deer.

Mule Deer

These blacktail are smaller than the average muley, and their most definitive characteristic is a totally or near totally black tail.

Antler structure is proportionately less massive too, not just in relation to frame and weight, but in conformation as well. Side by side with a Northern muley, blacktail racks seem not only small but a bit spindly. Blacktail racks do, however, have the classic "Y" forking of the mule deer.

While there is some debate about the blacktail's status on the scale of taxonomic hierarchy, most biologists feel that this deer doesn't yet classify as a separate species. This position is supported by the willingness of the mule and black-tailed deer to interbreed, which they will do if given the opportunity.

It is thought, however, that the blacktail may be a "developing" or "emerging" species, and that he may grow into a state of evolution and development truly distinct from the muley. In the same breath, neither you nor I, nor this book, will live to see that day in history.

In terms of species habits, black-tailed deer amount to mule deer that have learned to live in a whitetail environment. They are still basically muley, but they are adapting to life in thick forests, and behaving accordingly.

Muley Distribution

Mule deer are decided Westerners, inhabiting suitable terrain west of a line that passes through Amarillo, Texas, to Bismarck, North Dakota. With the inclusion of the blacktail, their populations extend all the way to the Pacific.

The northern limits of the muleys' range begin at the southern tip of Canada's Great Slave Lake. Traveling south, their populations extend to a point that includes the interior of Mexico as far as the City of Durango.

Mule deer are also found in the Baja peninsula and on several large islands off the Pacific Coast.

Deer Hunting

Life History

Although mule deer are far more gregarious animals than whitetails are, the birth process is a solitary one. Does leave the large groups of deer they have associated with throughout the winter and early spring and wander off alone. They commonly deliver in tall grasses or on the brushy margins of forests, dropping one fawn if it is their first delivery and two if they are older. Triplets are rather rare.

Fawns are born anytime from early to late spring, depending on the latitude. In southern California and the warmer reaches of Arizona, fawns are normally dropped in mid-April. In the northern Rockies, I have come across newborn fawns as late as June 1.

At first fawns feed exclusively on milk and spend most of the day sleeping in the tall grass or curled up under a log while their mother feeds nearby. By the end of the first week they are beginning to show interest in tender grass, and by the third or fourth week vegetation accounts for a substantial part of their diet.

Around the fifth week of their life fawns are strong enough to travel and fleet enough to escape possible danger. At this time does begin their annual migration, or continue on it if they have fawned while the move was under way.

As deer move into the higher elevations, the herd disperses rather than remaining in a recognizable group. Young does and yearling bucks stay at lower elevations, old does push on to near the edge of alpine country, and the big, heavy bucks travel the farthest, often summering in the rocky crags and grassy meadows that lie above timberline.

The herd remains thus spread out over a wide range until cold weather approaches and the first snows of fall powder the highlands. Then the downward migration begins.

The movement amounts to a common drift toward the river bottoms. Young does and yearling bucks reach the lowlands first and the big, heavy-racked males arrive last. These older, trophy-class muleys are literally driven from their summer ranges, either by the deepening snow at higher elevations or the approach of rut.

The mating period in the north begins around November and continues to mid-December. The behavior of the males is typical of all deer: they forsake their solitary ways and wander extensively, fighting with other males and harassing does.

Mule deer doe go through several successive heat cycles, making pregnancy close to a sure thing. Barren or "dry" does are quite rare and seldom number more than 1 percent of the mule deer population.

Until truly severe weather sets in, usually in early January, mule deer are rather widely dispersed throughout the foothills of major mountain ranges, feeding on whatever woody browse may be in the area and on the grasses of southern slopes that either blow or melt free of snow.

When the full fury of winter locks in, the entire herd of resident muleys moves to low river bottoms and yards to spend the balance of winter's worst weather.

Like Eastern deer yards, it is these river-bottom wintering areas and the amount of food they are capable of providing that are the determining factor in the number of mule deer a range can support. Although the summer home of a herd of mule deer may be hundreds of lush miles of mountain and meadow, for three months out of the year the entire herd must get their food from a relatively limited area.

Should there not be enough food, the youngest deer are usually the first to die because they are smaller than the older animals and can't reach the high limbs that are the last available food source along the path to starvation. In poorly managed Western wintering areas, browse lines or "high-skirting" will be quite evident.

Mule deer remain in the yards until the sun gains enough

Deer Hunting

strength to begin melting snow cover off southern exposures, and
to nurture spring grasses. This often takes until mid-April. At
this time, they leave their wintering grounds and move up to the
exposed ridges where they can commonly be seen by the
hundreds.

They gradually disperse as more and more snow melts. Bucks
head for the high country, and does wander off to drop their
fawns before or during their migration.

Southern mule deer behave in much the same way as Northern
deer, though their life processes begin earlier. Fawns are
dropped in April and mating occurs in August and September.

Although snow isn't a strong influence in their annual movements, migrations do occur as deer follow the increased precip-
itation and green grass of spring into the high country, then re-

*Muleys spend the warmer months feeding on the sunny slopes of the
high country.*

Idaho Fish and Game Department

treat to the warmer winter temperatures and resulting vegetative growth of the valleys.

True to Bergmann's Rule, Southern mule deer are generally smaller in frame than Northern animals. Horns are smaller too, and yearling bucks commonly sport spikes. This is thought to reflect the less nutritious foods common to arid regions, rather than differences in type or an emerging species.

Perhaps the most interesting thing about a muley's life is that his annual movements and physical response to his environment (antler growth, mating, migrations, etc.) are thought to be controlled more by temperatures than by increasing and decreasing daylight. This would amount to a natural safety device to ensure survival, since days in the mule deer's northernmost ranges grow quite long when the weather is still snowy and bitterly cold.

This same kind of insurance against the dangers of severe weather is reflected in pregnant does. Although a doe's physical condition may not be the best, it won't affect the condition of her fawns. All muley fawns are born strong and healthy, no matter what the health of their mother may be, and they are then better equipped to survive the West's late spring storms that often drop several feet of wet snow around fawning time.

Habitat

Like any wild creature, the muley needs food and cover to survive. Favored muley foods include the tender tips of virtually all the conifers, sagebrush, juniper, grasses, forbs, chokecherry, serviceberry, mountain maple, oak, dogwood, mushrooms, Oregon grapes, and almost any farm or orchard crop. Of particular importance to the mule deer are bitterbrush and mountain mahogany; these amount to a staple in his diet and are a critical source of food during the wintering period.

Cover to mule deer is more a matter of geography than of vegetation. They favor a broken country for hiding: steep draws, rock outcroppings, frequent hills, rills, cliffs, gulches, and cou-

Bitterbrush (pictured here) and mountain mahogany are staples in a mule deer's winter diet. This bitterbrush has been overbrowsed during the winter. Note the "high-skirting" caused by deer's reaching up to feed on their hind legs.

lees. They certainly will bed down in, feed around, and frequent places with vegetative growth, but they prefer that growth to be sparse rather than lush. Another thing I have noticed about these deer is that they don't seem to like deciduous growth for cover. They will occasionally make a bed in low-growing mountain mahogany or bitterbrush, but I have seldom jumped them in a lush stand of cottonwood or quaking asp. Conversely, they love to hole up under large, thick-branched ponderosa, piñon, lodgepole pine, and juniper, particularly when the trees are scattered around a mountainside rather than growing in close legions.

Although the mule deer is commonly thought of in terms of massive mountains that scrape the sky, they are also at home in the hilly ranchlands that are found several hundred miles east of the Continental Divide.

Plains habitat suitable to mule deer must meet those requirements common to the mountains: the land must be rough and broken and there must be some cover in the form of conifers or deciduous brush.

Because the muley's food source and environment are often dry in this situation, the availability of water becomes an important component of habitat here. But mule deer are willing to journey quite a distance to get it, so water holes spaced 5 to 10 miles apart are sufficient to support deer in an area.

Space—just wide-open, broad, unpeopled space—is also a habitat requirement for a muley. Unless they have plenty of it, they don't fare well, and I suspect there is something in their psychological makeup that puts them uptight when they are forced to live in close quarters or around too much civilization. They can tolerate the occasional inconvenience of a cowboy riding fence or the aimless wanderings of a hunter, but when humans become a permanent fixture, they move out.

I have seen this happen firsthand twice now: once when I built the cabin in which I now live and once when a tiny town boomed with the construction of a ski slope. In both cases, signs of deer in the area moved further back into the wilderness as human activity increased and persisted.

The idea that mule deer need space is further supported by their refusal to live in thick forests, even if frequent edge areas are logged into the otherwise unbroken timber. The shade of the forest and the close safety of lush undergrowth just aren't their cup of tea.

Strangely enough, though, they are also unable to cope with totally flat plains-type country. Even if there is a lot of "space" around, they want the rough geography of breaks and coulees.

These two types of unsuitable habitat, and the muley's reluctance to endure either, are cited by biologists as main reasons why the muleys haven't migrated beyond the borders of their current range in the West.

Mule Deer Habits

"Migrations" and the part they play in a muley's life deserve some careful explanation. Mule deer migrations don't approach the universality, size, or distances characteristic of elk or, more spectacular yet, caribou.

Generally the "herd" and its movement are confined to one drainage, and by that term I don't mean a major river drainage such as the Missouri or Columbia. Rather, these drainages will feed a small river or creek 5 to 10 yards across at its broadest point.

These creeks characteristically begin at high elevations, run for 15 to 20 miles, and drop several thousand feet before entering large agricultural valleys to empty into a major river. The total area they drain may be 100 to 150 square miles, and each drainage will have its resident "herd" of mule deer that remains within the loose confines of its borders.

These migrations, then, involve annual movements from the lowest country in a specific drainage to the higher alpine meadows and back. They are keyed and directed by weather and available food rather than an instinctual urge.

When the deep snow of winter first starts to melt, it does so at the lowest elevations first, exposing and nurturing fresh spring growth on the newly bared earth. As the days get warmer and the sun stronger, the receding snows pull back up the mountainsides and retreat up the creek bottoms into the high country. Muleys follow this progress of spring and green grass into the alpine meadows, then come down when the snows start to deepen and pickings get lean in the fall. This is the basis for their "migrations."

But even with the significant effect snow has on a muley's life, it is not that every deer in the neighborhood is poised at the edge of leaking snowbanks either. Muley movements are always more of a drift than an en masse stampede, a principle rather than an unalterable rule. This is also evident in the general behavior of the migrating deer.

The herding instinct is thought to be the evolutionary result of the need for protection. Herding is most common among animals who, like the muley, are creatures of the open rather than skulkers. When an animal chooses to live in open terrain, a herd provides a hundred eyes, ears, and nostrils to detect the approach of predators and alert its members to possible danger.

But personal experience has given me some severe misgivings about branding muleys as true "herd animals." Like their migrations, they do exhibit herding tendencies, but it is not a definitive life-style.

For example, herding in the mule deer isn't pronounced during the kind of weather you would expect of spring and summer. They will feed and associate in loose groups, but family units establish and abide by their own patterns. On the other hand, during periods of unusual stress and circumstances, such as storms of long duration, freak snows, yarding periods, and hunting pressure, they do indeed revert to herd behavior. At these times it is not unusual to bump into groups of twenty to thirty animals.

They react like a herd, too, in these large groups. When they first discover your presence, they appear to mill about and look for some sort of direction. Then a leader emerges—every time I have witnessed this, it has been a large doe. She is the first one to take flight, and a split second later the rest of the herd follows her lead, single-filing up a steep draw and over a hilltop, or into the maze of low-growing pines.

I haven't, however, seen the tendency to herd on the part of large bucks. In a group of thirty deer, there may be a few fork horns that will follow the leader, but if there are any really big racks among the deer—and I have seen this positively happen only during the rut—they bolt off on their own.

I think that I have also seen this performance during the winter yarding periods, but I can't be positive. Winter days in Montana are rather limiting in terms of a guy who likes the outdoors, and one way I break the monotony is to "hunt" deer on skis or snowshoes just to watch them at their—and my—leisure. Every time the herd has discovered my presence and hightails it out of the neighborhood, there are always a few deer that go a route of their own choosing, refusing to follow the pack. But because horns are gone by that time, and muscle structure is depleted by inactivity and low-quality food, I can't be sure that they are males.

Along with bringing about a more pronounced herding nature, hunting pressure will also push a herd of deer out of an area. Usually the muleys will retreat into more inaccessible regions and remain there until driven out either by renewed hunting pressure or by changes in the weather.

A muley's daily habits reflect the wide-open country he calls home. These deer, being creatures of the open, rely on a good view and their acute senses to reveal danger.

They seldom feed in the pitch dark, beginning their morning meal at first light. Feeding continues for one to three hours into the day. They feed in the middle of a pasture or on the open slopes of a hillside, rather than around forest perimeters or in hidden parks.

Because their favored summer and fall foods are rather dry, the feeding period at this time of year is commonly followed by a drink at the nearest water hole. In hot weather the drink may include a mud bath to repel flies. When there is snow on the ground, muleys eat it in lieu of drinking.

Mule deer bed down during the day, usually in a spot with a good overview. They also prefer the heads of draws, canyons, and coulees for beds because winds tend to blow up the bottom of these depressions, providing still another way to detect the approach of a predator.

Winter yarding areas are the critical determinant in the life cycle of the mule deer.

A typical mule deer bed is a small, flat dish in the earth, with a fast-rising bank or hill directly behind it. These beds are not in the bald open, but are thinly camouflaged by a few twigs of brush, tall grasses, or the trunk of a tree.

The same bed will be used frequently, though not always by the same deer. I would imagine it is a matter of there being just so many appealing and appropriate locations, so those that exist are used.

To feed, mule deer characteristically go downhill; to bed, they go up. The youngest deer—does, fawns, and yearling bucks—usually make their beds quite close to their feeding areas: under the brow of a small rise or on the side of a coulee a few hundred yards from where they fed. But the big bucks go further and higher, sometimes journeying many miles to find a place that offers both solitude and a panoramic view. They commonly go right to the top of a mountain, bedding down scant yards below its crest so they can hear danger coming from above, and see and smell it should it come from below.

Mule deer seldom feed at midday and seem content to remain in their bed until it is time for the evening feeding period. This begins two to three hours before sundown. On their way to their feeding areas, they amble along trails, nibbling at brush as they slowly move down. Several deer often feed together, and this is particularly true when they are munching on hayfields and wheatfields or other croplands.

After this evening meal even big bucks seem reluctant to travel long distances back to their daytime bedding areas, and commonly lie down quite close to the area where they fed. In the light from my car headlights, I have often seen some magnificent racks lurch to their feet along the side of some often driven ranch road.

Mule deer doe head a matriarchal unit consisting of two years' worth of fawn production, and one or two of those offspring could be young bucks. Because the muley is a marginal herd animal, several of these matriarchal units commonly feed together, and bed in the same general area at times other than the yarding period.

During the rut, bucks tend to follow does. Popular mythology has it that the "smarter" bucks make the does go ahead of them to test the water—to scout for the possible presence of hunters. From what I have seen of this, I think that it is more a matter of keeping a doe in sight and in scent, much as a male dog follows a bitch in heat.

Weather has a profound effect on mule deer habits, undoubtedly because its severity is more extreme in the mountainous West than in other areas of the nation. During the pleasant weather mule deer go about a rather normal day, feeding morning and evening and bedding during midday, but as a storm approaches they undergo a significant rise in activity. They feed later and earlier, occasionally feeding even in the middle of the day. Exactly what it is that keys this response is a matter of debate; some people feel it's the cloudiness and accompanying limited light that urge them to eat more heavily. I tend to believe that the deer are sensitive to changes in barometric pres-

The mule deer is a creature that loves broken ground—gulches, coulees, cliffs, steep hills—and, most of all, wide-open space.

sure, because I have often witnessed this increased activity when the sky was still clear, with only a few mare's tails to hint at the approaching storm. Whatever the reason, mule deer spend more time grazing and moving about before a significant change in the weather.

With the advent of either strong wind or rain, muleys disappear into the tall timber. This is the only time they will commonly be found bedded down in thick cover. Once the storm ends, a new period of high activity begins, even more pronounced than the one that preceded the nasty weather. After rain or a light snow, animals move to the nearest feeding grounds and spend long hours filling up on missed meals. Following a heavy snowstorm smaller bucks and does browse around familiar grounds for a day or so, then begin a gradual drift to lower elevations where they know that pickings will be easier.

Whether they remain at these lower elevations is determined principally by snow depths. If the storm was an early one and the snow will most likely melt from all but the highest peaks, muleys follow the retreating snowbanks back into the high country. This is especially true if they encounter significant hunting pressure at lower elevations.

If it's a late-season storm, and the snow from it will stick around until next spring, it will probably usher along major and permanent movements of deer into the lowlands.

Big bucks need more than one heavy snowfall to move them out from their lofty retreats. Usually the snow must be several feet deep and crusted before they drift toward the winter yards and easier living. Realize, though, that the time of year plays a part equally as important as the weather in their decision to migrate. If the rut is in full swing, they will search out the company of does no matter what their location or the condition of the weather.

The moon also influences mule deer behavior during hunting season. When it is full and bright, they revert to nocturnal feeding if they have been pressured by hunters.

Mule deer exhibit some interesting personal habits in terms of their reaction to danger. Like whitetail, they flare their rump hairs when alarmed. The view isn't so dazzling as the snow-white rump of a whitetail, but it is several shades brighter than their hairs appear at rest. Bright cream is the color that best describes it, and it readily shows up on a hillside of gray sage, while the rump's normal color blends in. Its sudden appearance will often reveal a deer you didn't know was there, as well as indicating that the animal is on the alert.

You can learn a lot about mule deer by watching their ears carefully. If they protrude from the animal's head at a near right angle, you are probably looking at a buck. The interference of their horns makes them carry their ears down further than a doe does.

Just before a mule deer runs, it lays its ears back, like a mule getting ready to kick or a horse that is feeling ornery.

When caught by surprise at close range, a muley's first reaction is to get some distance between you and it. It doesn't spend time sniffing, listening, or watching; it gets up and runs away. A muley simply won't tolerate potential enemies at close quarters.

Safety to a muley is uphill, and it can be depended on to head that way at every opportunity. If you are above a muley and surprise it, it may run downhill for a few yards to get some space between you and it, but then it will move laterally, usually with the wind, and cut back uphill as soon as it finds suitable cover such as a gulch or coulee.

A mule deer often stops at a range of two to three hundred yards and looks back, offering a perfect standing shot. It is my belief that this seemingly stupid move is part of its defense mechanism; it feels safety in distance, and once it has gained enough of it, it becomes interested in better identifying its pursuer. It can be encouraged to stop if you whistle or yell at it while it is on the run.

Deer Hunting

When it is being pursued, a mule deer can be counted on to travel in a relatively straight line. If you can keep an eye on its path for a hundred yards or more, you should have a good idea of the direction it is headed. A deer that has been jumped but not shot at will seldom travel more than a mile and a half before it beds down again. Jumped a second time or shot at the first time, a muley often strides out for 4 miles before bedding down.

Muleys are neither especially wary nor overly inquisitive. Rather than a dogged desire to identify every new feature of their environment, they are content to give new, unfamiliar objects a wide berth until they become accustomed to them. This is especially true of such things as horses, hunters, and pickup trucks. So long as they are far enough away to satisfy the deer, muleys will go about their business paying little or no attention.

All these habits are predictable to a point near foregone conclusion with the bulk of mule deer populations—fawns, does, and young bucks—and it makes them a lot easier to hunt than whitetail. But there is something of a "sucker" factor operating too. Hunters get so used to the behavior patterns of these animals that they begin to expect and depend on them. Then when an oddball comes along that doesn't behave according to Hoyle, hunters can't do anything right.

Those "oddballs" are usually the biggest of the bucks, explaining, perhaps, how they got to be mosshorns in the first place. And failure to anticipate their uncommon performance has cost me three monumental racks so far. How the biggest of the trio slipped through my fingers deserves retelling.

I was hunting late in the season near the Wyoming/Montana border on the ranch of an old friend of mine, Eli Spannagel. Eli's ranch is made up of two broad, high flats that form the divides between three separate drainages. Along their borders the ground sloughs off into a broken land of steep, timbered coulees that drain into rich hayfields and wheatfields miles below on the creek bottoms. Because of the proximity of ideal cover and easy food, Eli's ranch often turns up exceptionally large deer.

Our hunting technique was a common one in the West: we would drive a pickup truck to the head of a particular coulee, then work it out afoot. It had been productive enough in terms of numbers; we had seen better than a dozen animals that morning. But none of them packed the kind of rack I felt was needed to close the season out properly.

Then just before noon we drove out on the tip of a finger-like ridge that poked its way between two steep, narrow canyons of scrubby ponderosa pine.

"Might as well eat lunch here," Eli said. "Got a nice view to look at while we eat, then we can work off the food by walking." He killed the motor.

My fingers were just wrapping themselves around a ham and cheese sandwich when I noticed a deer watching us 50 yards down the slope.

Spotting a mule deer is always a slightly odd sensation. You would think it would be easy to see—a big animal in open country—but it is not. First you notice something out of place. Perhaps it's the buff-white of its throat or rump, a hint of movement, or an odd shape that doesn't fit in with the surroundings. You look closer and slowly it melts into perspective, taking shape and form as if viewed through a camera being brought into focus.

This one was pointed downhill, with his neck craned around toward us and his ears outstretched. Making up his mind that the pickup was something to be avoided, he swung his head back in line with his body and began striding off. It seemed that a massive, leafless tree followed the bob of his body.

I don't know how many points he carried; there were too many to count in the brief time I had a side view. But as he loped downhill, the regal V of his tangled antlers seemed too heavy for his head and dwarfed his large frame by proportion.

Deer Hunting

I hit the pickup door with my shoulder, rolling sharply to the bed in the rear where my rifle lay cased. Between the time the door sprung wide and I had my rifle up to my shoulder, the deer had seen enough to warrant a faster retreat. He now scratched out in long strides, heading for the bottom of the coulee.

At that point I had a fair shot. Nothing I would write in my diary, but if the animal had been a whitetail I would probably have taken it. He was between 70 and 80 yards away and running hard, straight downhill.

What really clinched my decision not to shoot was one of the neatest tricks I have seen a deer pull yet: he was running with his head so low to the ground that all I could see were the tops of his horns and a buff-brown butt. Besides, I thought, once he hit the bottom of the coulee he would turn uphill, affording a clear sideshot.

His hooves no sooner clattered on the rocky shale of the coulee bottom than he swung abruptly downhill, putting a sizable stand of branches and bushy pine between me and him.

"Damn that deer," I muttered and heard Eli chuckle in response.

The coulee to the left of where we were parked began as a very small cleft in the earth 30 yards behind the pickup, so I ran down to the bottom and up onto the next point of overlook in anticipation of the deer's cutting back uphill there.

When I finally found a view, the deer had outfoxed me again. He had turned uphill all right, but instead of following muley logic and the bottom of a gully, he had chosen a bare ridge for his ascent, turning right when I ran left. He was near the top, still running hard with a lowered head. At 75 yards it had been a tough shot; at 275 it was foolish to even consider.

But I had one ace left. He would stop and look back. I slid into a sitting position and set up for a steady rest. "Hey!" I yelled. The deer kept running. I flashed two fingers into my mouth and whistled long and shrill, then snapped back to the forearm of my rifle. Calling and whistling like that *always* gets a muley to stop.

The last I ever saw of him through my scope was a view identical to the first—cross hairs neatly centered on the south end of a deer heading north. He melted behind the ridgetop, never once behaving the way a muley is supposed to.

Hunting the Mule Deer

Three trophy-class bucks notwithstanding, muleys have a reputation with most hunters perhaps not for being outright stupid but for being less smart than the whitetail. It isn't really a matter of intelligence; muleys are an easier animal to hunt because their defenses are less effective against the natural inclinations and devices of man.

The most poignant example of this lies in their relative bedding habits. Whitetail choose tight brush where they are impossible to see, then rely heavily on their ears and nose to indicate approaching danger. It takes a master stalker to slip up on a bedded whitetail, and you seldom know he is there until he is up and off, dodging as if he were on a pogo stick.

Mule deer, on the other hand, prefer to bed in relatively open terrain, with only meager camouflage between them and the prying eyes of predators. They rely heavily on sight as well as sound and smell to reveal danger. This works effectively enough with the coyote and the mountain lion but isn't much defense against a man with a spotting scope and a long-range rifle.

Mule deer do have a few edges on human nature, though. First is the simple matter of accessibility.

Because they are a far-ranging animal, hunting muleys involves a lot of walking, most of it straight up and down. Many nimrods, especially those used to whitetail, have neither the energy nor desire to walk 4 to 8 miles a day over rough country. That in itself is a limiting factor: hunters have to go to the deer; they are not going to come to you.

In addition, shots at mule deer are often long. A 250- to 300-yard standing shot is quite common, and many hunters, not used to long-range shooting, are reluctant to try a shot at that distance, or are incapable of an accurate delivery.

I find this problem particularly acute in my work as a guide. Understandably enough, the bulk of the people who hire me are hunting muley for the first time. When they have been weaned on the close-in snap shots common to whitetail, getting them to accept a 250-yard shot strains their imagination. They usually insist on getting closer—and often blow a chance at big deer because of it. This precise situation has happened so often that I now encourage target practice at long ranges for newly arrived clients. I have noted some amazing facial expressions when these people realize they can, indeed, hit a 2-foot-square box at 300 yards.

Finally, locating deer in such a vast landscape is a nearly impossible chore for someone who has started "cold." Because they are essentially wanderers, deer can populate an area one day and be gone the next. Hunting pressure, weather, available food, and human activity can move them this way, then that, and unless you have a finger on the pulse of muley movements via a guide, a rancher, or a hunting buddy in the know, you are starting off with two strikes against you.

Hunting techniques for mule deer are tied to the type of country you are in. In sparsely timbered mountains, the most effective approach involves extensive glassing with a spotting scope or binoculars. The hunter or hunters climb to a high point with a panoramic view, then spend long hours examining the surrounding terrain.

• Glassing is most successful in the morning. At this time deer are likely to be out feeding and moving around, and are easier to see than when bedded down. Another factor that works in the morning hunter's favor is that deer go from feed to their bed, giving a hunter a fixed location and ample time to make his play.

Rather than stealth and patience, walking and careful glassing are the keys to bagging a mule deer.

The glassing process takes a little savvy, because the initial tendency is to move too fast. With every new patch of terrain under scrutiny, identify every detail firmly in your mind or you are guaranteed to gloss over deer. You also have to establish a pattern of examination or run the risk of covering the same area several times.

Two systems have worked for me. Where earth contours are plain, I like to work out small drainages, beginning at the little headwalls that dish out just under the crest of hills. I then follow their course down to the valley floor. As my examination descends, I trace feeder gullies and gulches up to their course, one at a time.

When I am faced with a rather flat hillside, I impose a kind of mental grid on the landscape, dividing it into blocks and taking those blocks one at a time.

Glassing with one thing on your mind—finding a deer—can become tedious. But it won't be if you make some attempt to interpret what you see. A small grove of bitterbrush may indicate a little spring and a watering spot. It may also be a feeding and bedding area. The scree of rock and rubble at the headwall of a gully is an unlikely place to find a mule deer, but the thick grass that grows in the moist coulee bottoms below deserves special attention.

Lying for long hours, just quietly looking, is a wonderfully quiet time too, one where you have an opportunity to become intimate with the infinite variety that is the Western landscape.

Gray cliffs of granite grow orange, pink, then tan, with the rising sun; shadows are gray and purple, and you learn to tell time by their length. There was a time when all trees were green to me, but now I know that they can be smoky gray, navy blue, and, at times, almost black.

As the sun warms the air, frost relinquishes its grip on the rocks cleaved apart the night before, and mighty towers clatter down, piece by piece, before your eyes. You come to grasp how mountain ranges are humbled by a tiny drop of water, how canyons are knifed deep by streams, and how the gentle wind on your cheek blasts even crags and cliffs into smooth submission.

Knowing and understanding how the land is put together is more than a pleasant exercise too; once you see a deer, you have to slip into position for a shot. A thorough understanding of the terrain that lies between you and an animal is the only way to pick out a route for the stalk that will bring you close to him without revealing your presence.

This is sometimes difficult to judge accurately because opposite hillsides often appear flat and featureless to the eye in full daylight. The foreshortening effect of magnifying optics compounds the problem. One trick I use with considerable success is to carefully examine shadows. Often, their length and position will reveal strategically located cover and terrain that would otherwise not be obvious.

When laying out a route in your mind, don't neglect the wind. In normal weather, winds in canyons blow up: up the bottom of the canyon and up the canyon walls. It is largely a matter of sun-warmed air rising. This would prescribe a stalk that follows a circular pattern, swinging upstream from the muley's position and looping around so the hunter comes down from above. Even if the wind isn't a factor, this notion of coming down from above is still the most effective of all muley hunting techniques.

Because these animals are keyed to looking for danger from below, they seldom pay attention to the land that lies above them. Then too, "up" to a mule deer is roughly equated with safety; should something spook it from any direction, its initial reaction is to run uphill, very possibly into your lap.

To some extent, by going high first you also turn tables on another favorite mule deer defense. Above the deer, it is you who has the superior view. You are in a good position to predict escape routes and cut the deer off, and a better position for a clear shot. Even your personal winds will be in your favor. Once you get your elevation, moving downhill doesn't use up a great amount of energy, so you won't have to worry that your accuracy will be thrown off by a heaving chest.

This type of stalk generates an electricity unlike any other. You are truly a hunter, bending your every talent and sensibility to slip up on a wild, keen-sensed, and able creature unnoticed. Success and failure hang in the balance of every chance breeze and footfall, and the intensity is so great that the entire world shrinks to a circle that encloses you, your quarry, and the obstacles between you. There is no more absorbing or exciting way to hunt, and don't be surprised if success turns out to be a bit of an anticlimax; it usually does with me.

While glassing is my favorite way to hunt muleys, it isn't the only method. There are times when glassing is neither practical nor possible. Topography often prevents a thorough examination of surrounding lands with optics, and a lot of country thick with muleys is also relatively thick with obscuring timber or brush. There is also the time of day; except for the sheer pleasure of watching deer, afternoons are not a good bet for glassing. At these times, still-hunting, driving, and posting are all possible alternatives.

All three techniques in terms of mule deer hunting are predicated on getting above your quarry first. Still-hunting, for instance, is a matter of getting high, then hunting down.

• For the most part, still-hunting is limited to the densest cover utilized by muleys: timbered bowls and canyons in mountainous country. To gain altitude, climb on the downwind side of the area to be hunted, then when you reach a point above the suspected location of deer, move into the wind for several hundred yards and begin your descent.

On the way up, concentrate on being quiet rather than watching for deer. When cover is available, stick close to it. Don't walk in plain view through open meadows or bare slopes, and try not to skyline yourself by climbing on the very crest of a ridge back.

Once you are in position, descend very slowly. Measure your progress one step at a time, sweeping the forest below you with your eyes. If the walk up took an hour, the walk down should take four.

Natural terraces are favorite bedding spots. Muleys will bed down close to their edge to get a good view of the land below them.

Tall, old, but sparse timber is another natural bedding area. Look for deer on the uphill side of the tree trunks.

• Driving is an extremely effective way to hunt mule deer, yet only a handful of hunters out West ever think to try it.

The technique works best when employed to work out a well-defined geographic area—a steep canyon, for example, rather than a flat-faced hillside. Two drivers are plenty for most muley drives; the deer are easy to move out and won't try to double back between the hunters.

Two men spread 200 yards apart can easily cover a quarter-mile-wide canyon. One man walks up high, close to the ridge, and the other walks in or near the bottom. As they go up, they don't have to be purposefully noisy, although it sometimes pays to roll rocks down through thick brush and any terrain that can't be seen by the walkers.

The natural place to post is at or near the head of the canyon, where its sides gentle out before reaching the mountain or ridgetop. Muleys, when pressed or frightened, tend to stick to the protection of sparse brush and timber, so posters are best located in a spot where they have a good view through, or down into, any nearby timber.

Like the stalker, posters must take a quiet, circuitous route up to their stands.

A driving and stalking combination makes for a pleasant way to hunt away a day. Organize a drive that covers one section of a mountainside in the morning, then move laterally, fan out, and stalk down in the afternoon. Or go right over the top and come down on the opposite side of the mountain.

• Ridge-running combines some aspects of still-hunting with some of glassing. It is a technique whereby one man can cover great expanses of ground in the course of a day.

When mountains are thrust up or canyons eroded away, water creates drainages that are bolstered by one central high divide —a kind of backbone.

Water drains down each side of this ridge, creating coulees, gulches, and gullies, with fingers of high land between the depressions. Viewed from the air, you would see a pattern predominant in nature, evident in the veins of a leaf, the growth of a stream, the blood vessels of the human body, and any mound of eroded earth from a sandpile to a mountain range.

By climbing to the top of a divide, a hunter is automatically above any deer in the area. Hunting is then nothing more than quietly walking out on each finger and carefully glassing the land below and the hillside opposite you. Virtually no feature of the terrain will be hidden from your view.

Because of a big buck's tendency to bed down up high, ridge-running rates as a top technique for the lone man after a trophy rack.

• Posting alone for a muley will work under certain circumstances, but for the most part a stand is going to amount to a lonely and unproductive vigil unless you locate it in an area where you know deer to be—and then you are often better off to hunt it by still-hunting, driving, or glassing.

Posting works best when deer migrate daily from feeding to bedding areas. This is a common situation when populations of mule deer live near agricultural land, and when heavy snows in the mountains drive deer to forest perimeters and they begin to feed in the bordering meadows and hayfields.

All the deer feeding in that area will follow essentially the same route to and from their beds. Once you find that route— the fresh signs should be quite obvious—all that is left to do is to secrete yourself somewhere along the trail morning and evening.

Mule Deer

• Hunting mule deer on horseback is a technique envisioned by a lot of hunters who have never chased muleys around the mountains. According to Dave Wolny, my partner in the guiding business, "put a pilgrim on a horse and you might as well give him a drum to beat in the woods."

His point is well taken; the myth that a muley is not afraid of a man on horseback is just that—a myth. Horses are far noisier and more obvious than a man could ever be in his wildest, most stumbling moments. Then too, gunplay and horses are bad business. A few mounts may not be bothered by the sound of gunshots, but for the most part horses get downright unmanageable when rifles are booming nearby. It goes without saying that shooting from the back of a horse is folly at its epitome; it is dangerous to the hunter, hard on horses since it kills many of them, and provides a steady rest for your rifle on a par with that of a small boat on a stormy sea.

Horses do have a place in the scheme of mule deer hunting: winding up some switchback trail with packs and hunters on their backs, skidding out carcasses, and snickering in the background of a high-country camp.

But in terms of actual hunting, leg work is the only kind of transportation that will pay off when you are after muley.

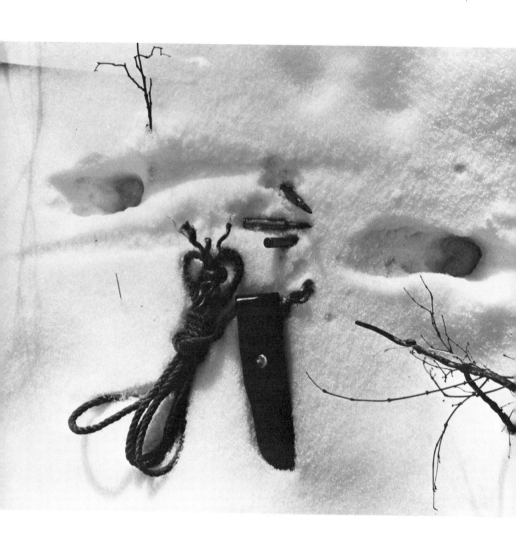

4
Skills, Savvy, and Equipment

ONCE YOU UNDERSTAND a deer's nature—its habits, defenses, and personality—you are in a position to predict its movements and reactions. You know how it goes about its daily life, what it will do if alarmed, and those places it is likely to be found at any time of day.

With that knowledge and any gun that shoots straight, you can go out and kill a deer.

But there is more to deer hunting than just that: a whole raft of associated skills and savvy that add breadth and depth to the sport.

In and of themselves, these things can be a source of personal satisfaction: I find an uncommon pride in carrying a knife I can shave with; in being able to place an effective shot; in knowing how to read the signs that lie hidden in wet grass, fall leaves, and the rubs on trees, and in being able to put them into meaningful order. And I have never met a deer hunter who didn't share that attitude.

But there is something in these skills that extends beyond self and knowledge for its own sake; they are a vital part of the total picture, essential components of the whole.

You don't have to know what a deer eats to kill one, or name a tree to sit in its shade. If someone else sharpened your knife, it will still cut for you. Yet when you can and will do these things on your own, you will discover a unique pleasure—you will become what you do.

It's a dimension of deer hunting that makes the experience richer yet, and a hunter wealthy in the bargain.

Buck Fever

Buck fever is considered to be the sign of an amateur—a beginner who gets so excited at seeing his first deer that he fumbles and fiddles around instead of getting down to the cool professionalism of an accurate shot.

I have seen some strange things happen with clients in terms of buck fever. One hunter from New Hampshire who had taken his share of whitetail, on seeing a rather nice four-point muley, squeezed his trigger so hard that his knuckle went white—and never thought to take off his safety until the deer had bounded away.

Another fellow on stand during a drive saw several deer coming toward him and bellowed out, "Here they come, boys!" He then proceeded to shuck every shell out of his lever-action carbine without touching a cap. And until he fully realized what he had done, he insisted that his gun wasn't working right.

There is no cure for buck fever that I know of, besides seeing a lot of deer in the woods. You simply don't know if you will be afflicted until that moment when you realize you are looking at a deer with your name on it.

At that time, if your heart starts to beat out a paradiddle, and your hands shake, and a flash of light and heat shoot to your brain, you might try taking a deep breath and talking yourself back into calmness. But it probably won't work.

There is no shame connected with the disease; if anything, it is a testimony to the incomparable excitement of deer hunting and your involvement in it. And I would suspect that anyone who has hunted deer has had it once or twice, though not everyone is willing to admit it.

Speaking for myself, I had "buck fever" when I shot that first white-tailed doe. And a very substantial dose of it when I shot the largest muley I ever saw, though not quite enough to completely bollux my shot. To tell you the truth, I think buck fever is a little like malaria; even though it's "cured," it returns often in minor attacks. I get those small attacks regularly—every time I meet a deer in the woods.

Placing the Shot

"Where's the best place to hit a deer?" is a question that invariably pops up in hunting-camp conversation.

"Heart . . . lungs . . . spine . . . neck . . . shoulder"—the battle lines are drawn around the wood-burning stove and the arguments lead into the evening.

In fact, there is no "best" place on which to superimpose a bull's-eye for all time. An effective shot in one situation may be the worst possible choice under other conditions, so before you squeeze a trigger, you have to make some judgments about what you want your bullet to do.

For example, a lung shot is a favorite among hunters, and rightly so. Of all the vital organs, the lungs present the largest target. Correctly placed, in the middle of the chest area and just behind the front leg, a lung shot ruins only a few ribs and amounts to a sure kill.

However, a lung shot doesn't kill immediately. You can expect your animal to run up to 100 yards, and perhaps even more. While this is of no concern on the plains of the West, how about a mule deer perched on a precipice in the mountains? Or a whitetail in extremely dense brush?

A running deer in both these situations may mean trouble. The whitetail may easily be lost in the heavy cover since with a lung shot there is often no immediate blood trail to follow.

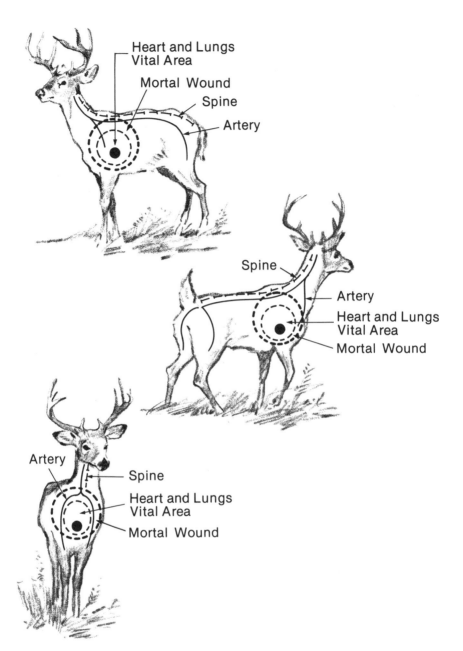

A shot in the spine or the vital heart/lung area will result in the quickest, cleanest kills. While it won't kill as quickly, severing a main artery or rupturing the area surrounding the heart and lungs amounts to a shot that will produce a mortal wound.

The muley may fall off the cliff and become hamburger, or run far downhill, making the drag out pure hell. In both cases, a shot that drops the animal in its tracks may be wisest.

This would mean breaking the spine. The most effective way to do this is by hitting the neck. The little meat that is lost is the least palatable on a deer anyway. The same results will occur if you connect anywhere along a line about 4 inches below the animal's back, but as you get further toward the rump area, you are shooting up some prime meat: chops and loin roast.

A head shot will, of course, poleax an animal, but it's hard on horns and skull if you are sighting in on something you may want to mount. A head also presents a rather tiny target; aiming at the neck, lungs, or back at least gives you some latitude if you are off a few inches.

A heart shot is tricky—again, you have a relatively small target, and an animal often runs as far when it has been hit in the heart as it does when struck in the lungs. Then too, should you waver too far in one direction you will hit the front legs or shoulders, among the poorest choices to my way of thinking.

A shoulder shot will drop an animal quickly, since it breaks down the whole front quarters. But it also breaks them up. In the classic shoulder shot, you can figure on throwing up to one-third of the usable meat away: shoulder steaks, ribs, and several roasts. I can't abide that kind of waste, so all my shoulder shots are mistakes, and I try to admit to them at the time.

Any other shot is bad news: it either destroys great amounts of meat or only cripples an animal who will probably die soon after, unharvested.

The question surely arises about the deer who doesn't afford a crack at those vital areas, specifically the whitetail who bounds straight away, waving good-bye with its white flag. Well, next time you put up a whitetail, watch it carefully. It doesn't follow an arrow-straight course, but rather bobs and weaves up and down and side to side. If you shoulder your rifle immediately and place your sights just to the side of, or directly above, the dazzling white patch, you can count on at least one quartering-away lung shot or a head/neck shot.

Tracking

The ability to track an animal, and the relative wisdom of doing so, are matters of mixed blessings.

The hunter who spends a few days a year in the woods is all too often enthralled by a fresh set of tracks in new-fallen snow. It is understandable—there, right before his eyes is proof positive that a deer recently passed that way. What is more, an animal has to be at the end of those tracks.

His usual reaction, then, is to start following the sign like a hound on trail, eyes glued to the blue pocks in the snow, while in fact he should be looking far, far ahead. When he finally comes to the deer's bed, and sees the snow kicked up by a running animal, *then* he looks around, usually about five minutes too late.

The woods-wise hunter, on the other hand, often uses tracks to help him get his deer. When he finds fresh tracks (a matter we'll get to in a minute), instead of marking those closest to him he looks for those farthest away. He can then travel from point A to point B, remaining on the trail, but with his eyes free to look around.

Tracking should be done as quietly and slowly as still-hunting, and even when it is done correctly there is still no guarantee that you will bump into the deer that made the sign.

It has been my experience that all species of deer are very much aware of the trail they leave in the snow and its possible implications. They take great pains to backtrack on the trail, swinging wide left or right, then circling back to bed down at a point where they can watch the path they made and anyone who may be following it.

Furthermore, mule deer swing uphill before bedding down,

140

so hunters must approach from below—obviously to the advantage of the deer. Whitetail usually swing through heavy brush before they settle in, using the crackle and crunch that are bound to come with the hunter as an extra alarm system.

There is, however, value in knowing some things about tracks beyond the possibility that they will lead directly to a deer. By determining age, direction, and a few facts about the animal that made them, you are often in a better position to predict its movements and reactions.

Aging a track is important in a broad sense because it provides clues to the number of deer in an area and the time of their movements—to and from feeding, for example.

The entire trick to aging any kind of track is based on nature's desire to set things right. Any natural object, from a grain of sand to a stone to a pine needle, has a position of ultimate stability. In other words, a rock roughly in the shape of a mound, with one rounded and one flat side, is in its most stable position when it is resting on the flat side. If you put it on its round side, gravity, water, a breeze, or an animal's foot will eventually tip it over on its most stable side, where it will then remain unless it is again disturbed.

On a far tinier scale, a deer's hoofprint sets many things out of their position of ultimate stability: small particles of earth, leaves, a pebble, a pine needle, and so forth. They return to their proper position a lot faster than a rock because they are more easily moved. A few drops of rain will do it immediately. So will a gust of wind or two. But before this happens, the disturbed earth has a "fresh" appearance.

Exactly how long it will take for this "fresh" track to become "old" and harder to spot depends on many things. Generally, on a calm, dry day I would estimate six hours. There are also no rules of thumb to tell the difference between a one-hour-old and a three-hour-old track on hard ground. It can be done, but it requires practice and dedicated observation, and the ability is all in being able to perceive how far nature has progressed in obliterating the track: how long it takes tiny grains of sand to tumble into place and an acorn to slip back into the natural scheme of the forest floor.

Tracks are much easier to age on soft, moist ground, and easiest in wet snow.

When a track is first made, it is letter-perfect, with sharp, clear lines of definition around its edges, particularly between the hooves. For five to ten minutes after imprint, the ridge between the hooves will be more than sharp; it will have a feathered appearance, caused by tiny particles of snow or earth poised on its edge.

After ten minutes the earth begins to dry and fall into the track or, if it is soaking wet, to fall from its weight and lack of support. Snow will either melt or evaporate.

After an hour, the sharp edge or corner around the sides of the print and between the toes begins to lose its sharpness and definition. This definition continues to be blurred at a slower and slower rate until the track degenerates into a mere pockmark several days later.

Dry powder snow makes aging a bit trickier, but again it is done by attention to detail. When powder snow is disturbed, individual crystals are sprayed out. These crystals, which are rather obvious to a trained eye, will evaporate within twenty minutes, giving the disturbed snow a smoother appearance than when the track was minutes fresh. After forty-five minutes to an hour the disturbed snow begins to settle and solidify, creating a very thin crust around the print that is obvious to a light touch.

The direction of a track is an easy matter to determine in all but deep snow. Just remember that the deer is headed in the same direction as its arrowheadlike tracks point. In heavy snow, you will be able to ascertain direction by means of drag marks.

When a deer walks, it doesn't prance, but shuffles along. As it starts into a step, it picks up its foot rather neatly, then slides it forward into the next place the foot will fall.

The general appearance this causes in deep snow is a long slash, a footprint, and a short slash. The deer is going in the direction of the short-slash side of the print.

Another way to tell direction is hoof entry into deep snow. If you examine the prints carefully, you will see that they tend to enter the snow at an acute angle: the point of the hoof is thrust into the snow rather than brought down straight. The direction of the hoof points is the direction in which the deer is headed.

The speed at which the animal is traveling tells the hunter how much a deer knows. If it is walking, you can assume that the deer is unaware of your presence. If it is striding, it is probably aware of you, but moving far enough ahead so as not to feel threatened. A running deer is almost always one who has had a close call with a hunter; it's a sign that you are probably not doing enough looking, but you still may be able to outfox the animal by playing on its habits.

Here, too, tracks tell it all. The spacing of a deer's track depends a lot on its size, but generally you will find walking prints about 2 feet apart. At a walk, a deer places its hind foot very nearly into the print left by its front foot, so general appearance seems to indicate an animal that is walking on its hind legs. The tracks left by a walking deer in soft earth or snow are quite well defined and perfect in formation. On hard ground, the tracks of a walking animal are very difficult to discern.

A striding deer makes tracks 3 to 4 feet apart. The tracks are also more offset than those of a walking deer, so you should be able to make out four separate prints. In addition, the fast pace of the animal finds its hooves sliding into place; on soft earth or snow, the slick sliding area should be around 2 inches long and directly behind the clear print. On both hard and slippery surfaces, there should be some spraying of duff, dirt, or

WALKING DEER

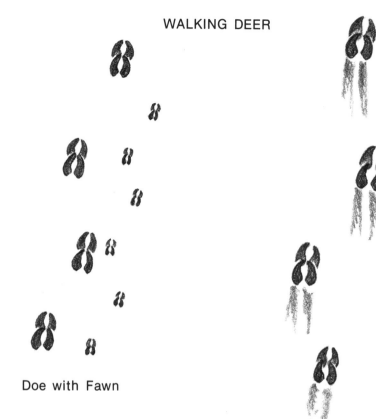

Doe with Fawn

At times other than the rut, a broad variety of hoofprint sizes made at the same time means a doe or does with fawns.

Buck with "Drag Marks"

In light snow, a buck normally drags his hoof tips before placing them firmly down. Note that hind feet fall very nearly into the print made by front feet, typical of both sexes when they are walking at ease.

STRIDING DEER

RUNNING DEER

The tracks of a striding deer are somewhat like those of a buck in snow, but drag or scuff marks will be evident even in dirt or mud as the hoof slides slightly before digging in. Note that dew-claw marks are more evident on a striding deer.

A deer on the run normally leaves two distinct prints at the head, and two in-line and often indistinct prints at the tail, of the track configuration. Track groupings can be as much as 15 to 20 feet apart when the deer is really scratching out.

snow around the track, also the result of the sliding of moving feet sliding into an abrupt brake.

A running deer is the easiest to define, because even on relatively hard earth its headlong flight and sharp hooves tear up quite a bit of turf every time it hits the ground. Look for a tight configuration of four prints, or disturbed snow or earth, 12 to 20 feet apart. Because of the way a deer places its feet when running, the configuration often looks triangular, with two prints at the base of the triangle and one at the apex. The base of the triangle points in the direction the deer is headed.

Ascertaining the sex of an animal through tracks is not so foolproof a proposition as some think. Though I have known a lot of nimrods who claim to be able to tell a buck from a doe by its tracks, I'm from Missouri when it comes to this area of deer lore, and frankly I have never been shown 100 percent reliability. There are some signs that point in the direction of a buck, though, and when you put them all together the odds say that you should be right.

• Size of the track is one indicator. A buck's track will be larger than a doe's; the prints will be deeper, longer, broader, and the space between strides will be greater. Realize, however, that a healthy four-year-old doe could well leave a larger print than a long yearling buck, so look for other signs to back up your hunch.

• Dewclaws are another hint. These are two hard, pointed appendages that grow just above the rear of the hoof. Dewclaws are usually more prominent in the print of a buck than in a doe's print.

• Drag marks are quite reliable when the snow is only 1 to 3 inches deep. Bucks tend to shuffle more than does and fawns do. In a skift of snow, this "buck shuffle" shows up as a slash in the snow surface leading to the print itself. The prints of does and fawns are clear, without any drag marks.

In deep snow, any deer will leave drag marks, but if you are sharp-eyed, you should be able to tell those deer that didn't pick up their feet by the depth and length of their drag.

• Another clue that points in the direction of male deer is step-cast. Straddle the track of a walking deer and look down the line of imprints. Does and fawns leave a rather straight path. Bucks throw or cast their feet outward as they move along.

• Urine provides still another check. When a buck urinates, his urine enters the snow at an acute angle to the direction he is traveling. A doe's urine enters the snow at an oblique angle.

Being able to track a deer isn't the most important skill you need in hunting, but it is a satisfying kind of knowledge that adds its dimension of intrigue and depth to the sport. It is quite important, though, when you have a wounded animal to contend with.

The first step to take when you think you might have wounded an animal is to establish that, indeed, you have. There are several clues that indicate a hit: sound, reaction, and hair.

When a bullet strikes flesh, you can usually hear the impact. It's a bit like a soft echo of the booming shot. An animal struck by a bullet should also show some signs: jumping straight into the air, hunching over, dropping its tail, appearing to stumble and fall, and so forth. Learn, too, to trust your instincts. When you are sure you hit that deer that seemed to get up and run away unscathed, you are usually right; there is a certain personal conviction that comes with an accurate shot.

The next step is to go to the area of impact, and there look for hair. When a deer is hit by a high-powered bullet, the explosive shock of contact cuts and jars loose hair—sometimes so much that the ground nearly looks like a barber shop. Realize, too, that the color and structure of the hair you find can provide valuable clues about where the animal was hit.

Look also for blood. It not only indicates a hit, but it can also tell you a lot about where the animal was struck and what it is likely to do.

Bright-red-orange to scarlet blood is that color because it is laced with oxygen. It is a sign of a clean hit, because that kind of blood comes from vital organs: the lungs, heart, and arteries.

Scarlet-to-cranberry-colored blood is less encouraging. It comes from veins and parts of the deer that carry a lot of meat. It usually means either a long tracking job or an animal that got away with just a scratch.

Realize, too, that the presence of blood is not a prerequisite to a hit. Many times external bleeding won't start until close to the time an animal expires. If you find hair, it is safe to assume that you have connected, and you must now follow up the animal.

The popular notion now is to wait for a half hour or so for the animal to "stiffen up" before you start on its trail. I personally feel this a foolish decision, largely because I have lost two animals by making it.

In the span of half an hour, blood will dry, become brown, and be much harder to see. Other signs—tracks, disturbed leaves and grass—will be less obvious, too. A half hour also gives the animal more time to cover ground and a chance both to get over the initial shock and doctor up its wounds, though it could easily die later.

So rather than waiting, I always get right on the trail, slowly and methodically investigating every possibility.

Pay particular attention to tracks; they can tell you a lot about where and how badly an animal was hit. The absence of one footprint in the four-print configuration indicates an animal with a broken leg. Blood around a footprint tells the lateral location of a shot. If it's a front foot, the deer was hit in the shoulder; a rear foot indicates a hit in the hams. If blood doesn't appear in footprints but is on the ground, the animal was hit in the neck or side.

Look for blood on brush. Its height will indicate the vertical placement of the shot. The amount of blood you find is important too. If you see a lot of bright blood, you can expect the animal to bed down soon in thick brush. Scant amounts of claret blood, or signs that a leg is broken with minimal bleeding, usually mean that a deer will head for water or mud. Deer roll and wallow in both to bind up their wounds.

As in any form of tracking, it is extremely important to keep your eyes on the terrain around you, not glued to the ground.

If you totally run out of sign, mark that point or spot with a hat or a handkerchief and begin fanning out in ever-widening circles, paying careful attention to thick brush. Often a deer will hole up in dense cover and die; when this happens it is just as hard to find as a downed bird.

If after an hour or so of searching, you find neither sign nor animal, you are safe to assume that the deer wasn't wounded that badly and has given you the slip. Deer are mistakenly portrayed as weak, delicate animals. In fact, they are quite strong and resilient; one buck shot in Montana was found to have a 10-inch stick in his lungs. At one time in his life he evidently ran into the sharply pointed object, and it punctured his side and broke off. Bones, flesh, and hair grew around the hunting-knife-sized piece of wood, and when the deer was killed he was in perfect health.

Rubs and Scratches

Rubs and scratches are made by all species of male deer in the fall. Rubs are the result of a male's either removing velvet from his antlers or polishing and sharpening them in preparation for battle.

By their mere presence rubs indicate bucks in the neighborhood, but the type of rub in evidence will give you some clues to the occurrence of rut, an important time in terms of the hunter after a trophy.

• All rubs are usually made on young trees, seldom more than 3 or 4 inches in diameter. They appear as a light spot on the

Velvet rubs normally occur in softwoods and are several feet off the ground (the knife indicates the size of the rub and tree).

tree, a place where bark has been rubbed and shredded free of the inner wood. Velvet rubs are higher than sharpening rubs, usually at the head height of the deer. Sharpening rubs are most commonly low, quite close to ground level; this is because of the angle at which a deer must tilt his head to get at the sharp points of his antlers. Velvet rubs are more concerned with the main beams.

Velvet rubs are also predominantly found on softwood trees:

A sharpening or fighting rub in a young hardwood. Note the fresh material on the snow; a buck aching for a fight is in the neighborhood.

pine, spruce, fir, hemlock, etc. Sharpening rubs occur on hardwoods: young maple, oak, hawthorn, and cherry.

• Scratches are the result of a male deer's pawing the earth, overturning duff, leaves, and sod, then urinating on the spot. They can be any size from that of a magazine to a medium-sized tabletop.

Scratches start appearing just before the rut, and they undoubtedly have something to do with mating. Exactly what is

151

another area of pleasant campfire conjecture involving the pale between popular myth and established fact. Some nimrods claim that a buck is staking out a territory, that he will ring his domain with the scratches as a warning to other bucks. Others feel that they are a kind of calling card for does, or perhaps a trysting spot. I am sure they have something to do with aggression or mating, for I have seen perfect parallels with male dogs around a bitch in heat. But beyond that, I shall keep my ideas to myself and reserve them for *my* debates around camp and hunting companions.

Dragging Out

Two "tools" are of irreplaceable value when you have to drag a deer to a pickup point: 10 feet of quarter-inch Manila hemp and a wide leather belt. Tie one end of the rope to the deer, the other end to the back of the belt, and you will be able to walk with both arms free, dragging your deer behind you.

There are a few tricks beyond that basic technique, however. First, always drag a deer from the head so it slides with the grain of the hair. If you try to go against the grain, you will need a Mack truck to budge the carcass.

It is also helpful to rig a makeshift harness around the head: a firm tie around the neck, then a half hitch around the nose. This keeps the head pointed in the direction you are going, and it is less likely to hang up on logs and brush.

Another trick that prevents hang-ups is to tie the two front legs behind the head in the conventional police-search posture. The carcass then amounts to a straight, streamlined package, and snakes through the narrowest path with ease.

There are times when dragging is either impractical or impossible. In thick, blown-down timber or on bare, hard earth, dragging creates more work than it saves. The same thing is true whenever you have to move a carcass uphill. If you find yourself in these situations, it is most practical to carry the deer bodily.

By tying each hind leg to each foreleg just below the first joint, you will have makeshift "pack straps" to slip your arms through and carry the animal on your back. This trick is largely limited to small deer and, during the gun season, is downright dangerous unless you cover the carcass with a red cloth or jacket.

A pack frame is another possibility. Should you down a deer far in the outback, it sometimes makes the most sense to skin and quarter the animal, then pack it out in two or three trips with the meat lashed to the frame.

Horses are often used to get game out of rough country. If the deer is too large to be packed out whole, cut it in half,

When dragging is difficult, nothing beats a wheeled platform for getting a downed deer out of the woods.

Michigan Department of Natural Resources

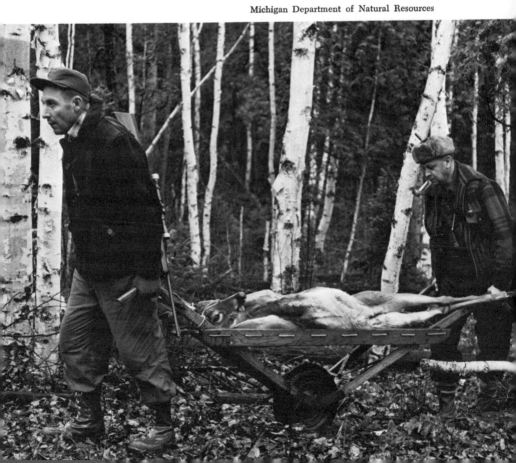

separating hind from front quarters by cutting through the backbone between the second and third ribs. This assures equal weighting of both pieces, and the ribs on the hindquarters amount to a handle to which a rope can be tied.

Situations that require the use of horses and packboards don't occur too often. As a rule, it makes more sense to get a deer out of a rough spot with the help of a hunting buddy.

Because the components are available, the most common way to do this is to lash a deer to a stout sapling. Lift each end of the sapling to a shoulder, and you and your companion are off through the woods. When tying the deer in place, get the sapling as close to the animal's center of gravity as you can and tie its head up. If you don't do this, the carcass will sway from side to side as you walk, making progress—and keeping your balance—difficult, to say the least.

A stretcher is a slightly better arrangement than a pole. It can be made on the spot with two saplings inside two buttoned jackets, or it can be a standard piece of equipment around camp.

An even more efficient device to have around a permanent deer camp is a wheeled stretcher. This consists of a light platform (usually plywood), roughly the dimensions of a stretcher, with handles on all four corners. A wheel, usually from a small child's bicycle, is mounted and braced in the very center of the platform. On flat, smooth terrain, the platform can be wheeled like a cart. When blowdowns and rocky ground prevent easy rolling, it is a cinch to lift the deer and the dolly around sharp corners and over obstacles.

The Dilemma of a Horn

If hunters would allow themselves a few moments of quiet introspection, I have absolute faith they would discover that they hunt for many more reasons than to shoot a deer. But things in the forefront of one's mind have a way of bubbling out to the exclusion of everything else—and to listen to a bunch of deer hunters in a card game, you would think that even the deer was immaterial; what they want more than anything else is horns!

There are many things that can be done with horns: they can be mounted, made into buttons, jewelry, knife handles, and so on. Speaking for myself, I like horns and occasionally shoot deer that own them. But they account for such a small part of the total concept of hunting and using a deer that I resent this adulation. While I don't exactly feel that it is a mortal sin to worship horns, I can't help sensing some connection between them and an incident involving a golden calf a few years back.

Along with that piece of cracker-barrel philosophy, I also find that humans have a habit of complicating things that are very important to them, especially if those things are basically simple.

I think I could produce some viable illustrations in the areas of government, law, and religion to support my case. I know I can in terms of deer hunting: those same horns.

Eastern count, Western count, typical, nontypical, mule deer, whitetail—these are all considerations made when you are sizing up horns.

• Eastern count means that you total up all the points on a deer's rack over an inch long. That includes the "eye guards" or "brow tines" that grow just above the point where the antler emerges from a whitetail's head. Note, I said "whitetail." There are no mule deer in the East, and even if there were, their brow tines wouldn't count. You don't include them when measuring up a muley.

• Western count means that you total up all the points on the heaviest side of the rack—the one with the most points over an inch long—and count only them. A deer with three tines on each side would be a "three point." One with three points on one side and four on the other would be a "four point." When totaling, you count the brow tines if you have shot a Western whitetail; you don't if you have a mule deer.

Unfortunately, there is no line of demarcation for "Eastern count" to end and "Western count" to begin. In Minnesota it is definitely an Eastern tally, in Montana absolutely Western, but things get sticky around Bismarck, North Dakota.

I have a solution to this particular problem: score all whitetail by Eastern count and all muley by Western count. As a matter of fact, I regularly do just that. Unfortunately, I am the only one I know of who has adopted the system, so there is some confusion when I hunt in Idaho and tell my partners I shot a ten-point whitetail, then show up with what they consider a five-point.

• Typical versus nontypical racks are a little easier to understand, and their definition a bit more uniform. A typical rack is one with equal points on both sides that boasts a degree of symmetry; one side of the rack is essentially a mirror image of the other.

A nontypical rack either has unequal points on each side or freakish symmetry with tines angling this way, then that, like a twisted bristle of barbed wire.

Horned does and stags occasionally occur in nature. Does grow wispy horns, usually spikes, if they have a certain kind of hormonal imbalance. This imbalance is quite rare; its probability of occurrence is about 1 in 18,000.

Horned does are incapable of breeding and are perfectly legal game even in a "bucks only" area. Laws usually cite "horned animals" rather than "males." Even if laws don't exactly read that way, game wardens are quite understanding in this situation.

If any sex or size of deer should be called a prize, I would say it is a stag. These are male animals whose testicles have been removed by accident or design. In nature they can be removed during a fight with another male or snagged when jumping a fence. Out West, cowboys occasionally lasso a young buck and castrate him like a bull calf. The result is equivalent to the effect produced in a steer: a huge frame that carries a lot of meat. In addition, this meat is the best-eating venison there is, tender and fine rather than muscular. Stags normally grow huge horns too, but they are usually nontypical, and always in velvet.

The Boone and Crockett Club is an organization of sportsmen united for the purpose of recording and cataloging trophy game animals. Because their scoring must be precise, horn measurements for the four types of North American deer are rather involved.

If you think you have downed a trophy, see pages 158 to 165 to measure your animal against their established standards.

Guides

Guides are advisable—and sometimes required of nonresidents by law—when you are hunting muleys in the mountains of the West. The chances of getting lost are part of the reason why, and so is the matter of being able to get into the vast backcountry and camp there comfortably and safely. Most out-of-staters have neither the knowledge nor the equipment needed to do this.

No matter where or what you are hunting, however, hiring a guide is worth considering. Because he is a professional, his vast store of knowledge is bound to increase your chances of getting game, even if you are hunting in your own state and in familiar territory. More important, though, his knowledge extends far beyond finding a deer; your guide can show you the subtle signs to take into account when aging a track and can point to the difference between the clipped brush of a rabbit on feed and the chewed ends of deer browse. Plant species, changes in cloud patterns and what they mean, and how to cook a fresh-killed grouse over an open fire—all these things and more are at the fingertips of a real professional, and when you hire him you will have them at your disposal too. A guide will

RECORDS OF NORTH AMERICAN
BIG GAME COMMITTEE

BOONE AND CROCKETT CLUB

Boone and Crockett Club
Records of North American Big Game Committee
c/o Carnegie Museum
4400 Forbes Ave. Pittsburgh, Pa. 15213

Minimum Score: Deer
Whitetail: Typical 170
Coues: Typical 110

WHITETAIL and COUES DEER

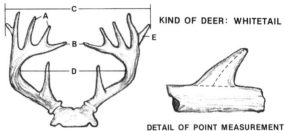

KIND OF DEER: WHITETAIL

DETAIL OF POINT MEASUREMENT

SEE OTHER SIDE FOR INSTRUCTIONS		Supplementary Data	Column 1	Column 2	Column 3	Column 4
		R. / L.	Spread Credit	Right Antler	Left Antler	Difference
A. Number of Points on Each Antler		6 / 8				
B. Tip to Tip Spread		9 2/8				
C. Greatest Spread		23 4/8				
Inside Spread	19 6/8	Spread credit may equal but not	19 6/8			
D. of MAIN BEAMS		exceed length of longer antler				
IF Inside Spread of Main Beams exceeds longer antler length, enter difference						
E. Total of Lengths of all Abnormal Points						5 7/8
F. Length of Main Beam				28 2/8	27 6/8	4/8
G-1. Length of First Point, if present				3 7/8	3 6/8	1/8
G-2. Length of Second Point				10 6/8	12 1/8	1 3/8
G-3. Length of Third Point				11 3/8	11 6/8	3/8
G-4. Length of Fourth Point, if present				10	9	1
G-5. Length of Fifth Point, if present				5	4 5/8	3/8
G-6. Length of Sixth Point, if present						
G-7. Length of Seventh Point, if present						
Circumference at Smallest Place H-1. Between Burr and First Point				5	5	
Circumference at Smallest Place H-2. Between First and Second Points				4 7/8	4 7/8	
Circumference at Smallest Place H-3. Between Second and Third Points				5 3/8	5 1/8	2/8
Circumference at Smallest Place between Third and Fourth Points or half way between Third Point and H-4. Beam Tip if Fourth Point is missing				4 6/8	4 5/8	1/8
TOTALS			19 6/8	89 2/8	88 5/8	10

ADD	Column 1	19 6/8	Exact locality where killed Starr County, Texas
	Column 2	89 2/8	Date killed 1945 By whom killed Unknown — Pick-up
	Column 3	88 5/8	Present owner Jack F. Quist
	Total	197 5/8	Address 8801 Bridgeport, Austin, Texas 78753
Subtract Column 4		10	Guide's Name and Address None
FINAL SCORE		187 5/8	Remarks: (Mention any abnormalities) Rack was thrown away by hunter and retrieved by Mr. Quist.

I certify that I have measured the above trophy on   *March 1*   19   71
at (address)   *Carnegie Museum*   City   *Pittsburgh*   State   *Pa.*
and that these measurements and data are, to the best of my knowledge and belief,
made in accordance with the instructions given.
Witness: *Charles E. Wilson, Jr.*   Signature: *B. A. Fashingbauer*
                              Boone and Crockett Official Measurer

Instructions

All measurements must be made with a flexible steel tape to the nearest one-eighth of an inch. Wherever it is necessary to change direction of measurement, mark a control point and swing tape at this point. To simplify addition, please enter fractional figures in *eighths*. Official measurements cannot be taken for at least sixty days after the animal was killed. *Please submit photographs.*

Supplementary Data measurements indicate conformation of the trophy, and none of the figures in Lines A, B and C are to be included in the score. Evaluation of conformation is a matter of personal preference. Excellent but nontypical Whitetail Deer heads with many points shall be placed and judged in a separate class.

A. Number of Points on Each Antler. To be counted a point, a projection must be at least one inch long AND its length must exceed the length of its base. All points are measured from tip of point to nearest edge of beam as illustrated. *Beam tip is counted as a point but not measured as a point.*

B. Tip to Tip Spread measured between tips of Main Beams.

C. Greatest Spread measured between perpendiculars at right angles to the center line of the skull at widest part, whether across main beams or points.

D. Inside Spread of Main Beams measured at right angles to the center line of the skull at widest point between main beams. Enter this measurement again in "Spread Credit" column if it is less than or equal to the length of longer antler.

E. Total of Lengths of all Abnormal Points. Abnormal points are generally considered to be those nontypical in shape or location.

F. Length of Main Beam measured from lowest outside edge of burr over outer curve to the most distant point of what is, or appears to be, the main beam. The point of beginning is that point on the burr where the center line along the outer curve of the beam intersects the burr.

G-1-2-3-4-5-6-7. Length of Normal Points. Normal points project from main beam. They are measured from nearest edge of main beam over outer curve to tip. To determine nearest edge (top edge) of beam, lay the tape along the outer curve of the beam so that the top edge of the tape coincides with the top edge of the beam on both sides of the point. Draw line along top edge of tape. This line will be base line from which point is measured.

H-1-2-3-4. Circumferences—If first point is missing, take H-1 and H-2 at smallest place between burr and second point.

Trophies Obtained Only by Fair Chase May Be Entered in Any Boone and Crockett Club Big Game Competition

To make use of the following methods shall be deemed UNFAIR CHASE and unsportsmanlike, and any trophy obtained by use of such means is disqualified from entry in any Boone and Crockett Club big game competition:

I. Spotting or herding game from the air, followed by landing in its vicinity for pursuit;

II. Herding or pursuing game with motor-powered vehicles;

III. Use of electronic communications for attracting, locating or observing game, or guiding the hunter to such game.

I certify that the trophy scored on this chart was not taken in UNFAIR CHASE as defined above by the Boone and Crockett Club.

I certify that it was not spotted or herded by guide or hunter from the air followed by landing in its vicinity for pursuit, nor herded or pursued on the ground by motor-powered vehicles.

I further certify that no electronic communications were used to attract, locate, observe, or guide the hunter to such game; and that it was taken in full compliance with the local game laws or regulations of the state, province or territory.

Date _____ Hunter _____

OFFICIAL SCORING SYSTEM FOR NORTH AMERICAN BIG GAME TROPHIES

RECORDS OF NORTH AMERICAN BIG GAME COMMITTEE
☐ NON-TYPICAL WHITETAIL DEER   Min. Score 195
☐ NON-TYPICAL COUES DEER   Min. Score 105:15 = 120

BOONE AND CROCKETT CLUB

Boone and Crockett Club
Records of North American Big Game Committee
c/o Carnegie Museum
4400 Forbes Ave. Pittsburgh, Pa. 15213

☒ NON-TYPICAL WHITETAIL DEER
☐ NON-TYPICAL COUES DEER

DETAIL OF POINT MEASUREMENT

ABNORMAL Points Line E	
R	L
10 5/8	10 7/8
7 6/8	6 6/8
6	7 2/8
2 2/8	9 2/8
Totals 26 5/8	34 1/8
To E	60 6/8

SEE OTHER SIDE FOR INSTRUCTIONS

	Supplementary Data	Column 1	Column 2	Column 3	Column 4
	R. L.	Spread Credit	Right Antler	Left Antler	Difference
A. Number of Points on Each Antler	9 | 9				
B. Tip to Tip Spread	8 3/8				
C. Greatest Spread	25 1/8				
D. Inside Spread of MAIN BEAMS 19 5/8 Spread credit may equal but not exceed length of longer antler		19 5/8			
IF Inside Spread of Main Beams exceeds longer antler length, enter difference					
E. Total of Lengths of all Abnormal Points	60 6/8				
F. Length of Main Beam			25 6/8	28 3/8	2 5/8
G-1. Length of First Point, if present			8 2/8	9 5/8	1 3/8
G-2. Length of Second Point			14 2/8	15 1/8	7/8
G-3. Length of Third Point			12 1/8	11 5/8	4/8
G-4. Length of Fourth Point, if present			6 4/8	5 7/8	5/8
G-5. Length of Fifth Point, if present					
G-6. Length of Sixth Point, if present					
G-7. Length of Seventh Point, if present					
H-1. Circumference at Smallest Place Between Burr and First Point			5 3/8	5 6/8	3/8
H-2. Circumference at Smallest Place Between First and Second Points			4 7/8	4 4/8	3/8
H-3. Circumference at Smallest Place Between Second and Third Points			6	5 2/8	6/8
H-4. Circumference at Smallest Place Between Third and Fourth Points			5	5	
TOTALS		60 6/8	19 5/8	88 1/8	91 1/8	7 4/8

ADD	Column 1	19 5/8	Exact locality where killed West Fork Milk R.—North Hill Co., Mont.
	Column 2	88 1/8	Date killed 11-10-68 By whom killed Frank A. Pleskac
	Column 3	91 1/8	Present owner Frank A. Pleskac
	Total	198 7/8	Address Simpson Route, Box 60, Havre, Montana 59501
Subtract Column 4		7 4/8	Guide's Name and Address None
Result		191 3/8	Remarks: (Mention any abnormalities)
Add Line E Total		60 6/8	Abnormal point from main beam below first point.
FINAL SCORE		252 1/8	

I certify that I have measured the above trophy on   *March 1*   19 *71*
at (address)   *Carnegie Museum*   City   *Pittsburgh*   State   *Pa.*
and that these measurements and data are, to the best of my knowledge and belief,
made in accordance with the instructions given.

Witness: *Charles E. Wilson, Jr.*   Signature: *B. A. Fashingbauer*
                                            Boone and Crockett Official Measurer

Instructions

All measurements must be made with a flexible steel tape to the nearest one-eighth of an inch. Wherever it is necessary to change direction of measurement, mark a control point and swing tape at this point. To simplify addition, please enter fractional figures in *eighths.* Official measurements cannot be taken for at least sixty days after the animal was killed. *Please submit photographs.*

Supplementary Data measurements indicate conformation of the trophy, and none of the figures in Lines A, B and C are to be included in the score. Evaluation of conformation is a matter of personal preference.

A. Number of Points on Each Antler. To be counted a point, a projection must be at least one inch long AND its length must exceed the length of its base. All points are measured from tip of point to nearest edge of beam as illustrated. Beam tip is counted as a point but not measured as a point.

B. Tip to Tip Spread measured between tips of main beams.

C. Greatest Spread measured between perpendiculars at right angles to the center line of the skull at widest part whether across main beams or points.

D. Inside Spread of Main Beams measured at right angles to the center line of the skull at widest point between main beams. Enter this measurement again in "Spread Credit" column if it is less than or equal to the length of longer antler.

E. Total of Lengths of all Abnormal Points. Abnormal points are considered to be those nontypical in shape or location. It is very important, in scoring nontypical heads, to determine which points are to be classed as normal and which are not. To do this, study carefully the character of the normal points on the diagram, which are marked G-1, G-2, G-3, etc. On the trophy to be scored, the points which correspond to these are measured as normal. *All others over one inch in length (See A, above) are considered abnormal.* Various types of abnormal points are shown (marked with an E) on the diagram. Measure the exact length of each abnormal point, over the outer curve, from the tip to the nearest edge of the beam or point from which it projects. Then add these lengths and enter the total in the space provided.

F. Length of Main Beam measured from lowest outside edge of burr over outer curve to the most distant point of what is, or appears to be, the main beam. The point of beginning is that point on the burr where the center line along the outer curve of the beam intersects the burr.

G-1-2-3-4-5-6-7. Length of Normal Points. Normal points project from main beam. They are measured from nearest edge of main beam over outer curve to tip. To determine nearest edge (top edge) of beam, lay the tape along the outer curve of the beam so that the top edge of the tape coincides with the top edge of the beam on both sides of the point. Draw line along top edge of tape. This line will be base line from which point is measured.

H-1-2-3-4. Circumferences—If first point is missing, take H-1 and H-2 at smallest place between burr and second point. If fourth point is missing, take H-4 half way between third point and beam tip.

Trophies Obtained Only by Fair Chase May Be Entered
in Any Boone and Crockett Club Big Game Competition

To make use of the following methods shall be deemed UNFAIR CHASE and unsportsmanlike, and any trophy obtained by use of such means is disqualified from entry in any Boone and Crockett Club big game competition:

I. Spotting or herding game from the air, followed by landing in its vicinity for pursuit;

II. Herding or pursuing game with motor-powered vehicles;

III. Use of electronic communications for attracting, locating or observing game, or guiding the hunter to such game.

I certify that the trophy scored on this chart was not taken in UNFAIR CHASE as defined above by the Boone and Crockett Club.

I certify that it was not spotted or herded by guide or hunter from the air followed by landing in its vicinity for pursuit, nor herded or pursued on the ground by motor-powered vehicles.

I further certify that no electronic communications were used to attract, locate, observe, or guide the hunter to such game; and that it was taken in full compliance with the local game laws or regulations of the state, province or territory.

Date   *July 22, 1969*   Hunter   *Frank A. Pleskac*

OFFICIAL SCORING SYSTEM FOR NORTH AMERICAN BIG GAME TROPHIES

RECORDS OF NORTH AMERICAN
BIG GAME COMMITTEE

BOONE AND CROCKETT CLUB

Minimum Score: Deer
Col. Blacktail: Typical — 130
Mule: Typical — 195

MULE and BLACKTAIL DEER

Boone and Crockett Club
Records of North American Big Game Committee
c/o Carnegie Museum
4400 Forbes Ave. Pittsburgh, Pa. 15213

KIND OF DEER: MULE

DETAIL OF POINT MEASUREMENT

SEE OTHER SIDE FOR INSTRUCTIONS		Supplementary Data		Column 1	Column 2	Column 3	Column 4
		R.	L.	Spread	Right	Left	
A. Number of Points on Each Antler		5	6	Credit	Antler	Antler	Difference
B. Tip to Tip Spread		24 3/8					
C. Greatest Spread		30 4/8					
Inside Spread D. of MAIN BEAMS	26 5/8	Spread credit may equal but not exceed length of longer antler		26 5/8			
IF Inside Spread of Main Beams exceeds longer antler length, enter difference							
E. Total of Lengths of all Abnormal Points							2 7/8
F. Length of Main Beam					26 7/8	28	1 1/8
G-1. Length of First Point, if present					2	2 1/8	1/8
G-2. Length of Second Point					20 2/8	20 1/8	1/8
G-3. Length of Third Point, if present					10 7/8	9 6/8	1 1/8
G-4. Length of Fourth Point, if present					13 4/8	13 7/8	3/8
Circumference at Smallest Place H-1. Between Burr and First Point					5 3/8	5 3/8	
Circumference at Smallest Place H-2. Between First and Second Points					4 6/8	4 6/8	
Circumference at Smallest Place H-3. Between Main Beam and Third Point					4 2/8	4 3/8	1/8
Circumference at Smallest Place H-4. Between Second and Fourth Points					5 4/8	5	4/8
TOTALS				26 5/8	93 3/8	93 3/8	6 3/8

ADD	Column 1	26 5/8	Exact locality where killed S. Indian Canyon, Lincoln Co., Wyo.
	Column 2	93 3/8	Date killed 11-13-69 By whom killed Al Firenze, Sr.
	Column 3	93 3/8	Present owner Al Firenze, Sr.
	Total	213 3/8	Address 1001 Airport Blvd. South, San Francisco, Calif. 94080
Subtract Column 4		6 3/8	Guide's Name and Address Monty Nelson, Alpine, Wyoming
FINAL SCORE		207	Remarks: (Mention any abnormalities)

I certify that I have measured the above trophy on   *March 2*   19   71
at (address)   *Carnegie Museum*   City   *Pittsburgh*   State   *Pa.*
and that these measurements and data are, to the best of my knowledge and belief,
made in accordance with the instructions given.

Witness: *Peter Haupt*   Signature: *Arnold O. Haugen*
                                            Boone and Crockett Official Measurer

Instructions

All measurements must be made with a flexible steel tape to the nearest one-eighth of an inch. Wherever it is necessary to change direction of measurement, mark a control point and swing tape at this point. To simplify addition, please enter fractional figures in *eighths.* Official measurements cannot be taken for at least sixty days after the animal was killed. *Please submit photographs.*

Supplementary Data measurements indicate conformation of the trophy, and none of the figures in Lines A, B and C are to be included in the score. Evaluation of conformation is a matter of personal preference. Excellent but nontypical Mule Deer heads with many points shall be placed and judged in a separate class.

A. Number of Points on Each Antler. To be counted a point, a projection must be at least one inch long AND its length must exceed the length of its base. All points are measured from tip of point to nearest edge of beam as illustrated. *Beam tip is counted as a point but not measured as a point.*

B. Tip to Tip Spread measured between tips of main beams.

C. Greatest Spread measured between perpendiculars at right angles to the center line of the skull at widest part whether across main beams or points.

D. Inside Spread of Main Beams measured at right angles to the center line of the skull at widest point between main beams. Enter this measurement again in "Spread Credit" column if it is less than or equal to the length of longer antler.

E. Total of Lengths of all Abnormal Points. Abnormal points are generally considered to be those nontypical in shape or location.

F. Length of Main Beam measured from lowest outside edge of burr over outer curve to the tip of the main beam. The point of beginning is that point on the burr where the center line along the outer curve of the beam intersects the burr.

G-1-2-3-4. Length of Normal Points. Normal points are the brow (or first) and the upper and lower forks as shown in illustration. They are measured from nearest edge of beam over outer curve to tip. To determine nearest edge (top edge) of beam, lay the tape along the outer curve of the beam so that the top edge of the tape coincides with the top edge of the beam on both sides of the point. Draw line along top edge of tape. This line will be base line from which point is measured.

H-1-2-3-4. Circumferences—If first point is missing, take H-1 and H-2 at smallest place between burr and second point. If third point is missing, take H-3 half way between the base and tip of second point. If the fourth point is missing, take H-4 half way between the second point and tip of main beam.

Trophies Obtained Only by Fair Chase May Be Entered in Any Boone and Crockett Club Big Game Competition

To make use of the following methods shall be deemed UNFAIR CHASE and unsportsmanlike, and any trophy obtained by use of such means is disqualified from entry in any Boone and Crockett Club big game competition:

I. Spotting or herding game from the air, followed by landing in its vicinity for pursuit;

II. Herding or pursuing game with motor-powered vehicles;

III. Use of electronic communications for attracting, locating or observing game, or guiding the hunter to such game.

I certify that the trophy scored on this chart was not taken in UNFAIR CHASE as defined above by the Boone and Crockett Club.

I certify that it was not spotted or herded by guide or hunter from the air followed by landing in its vicinity for pursuit, nor herded or pursued on the ground by motor-powered vehicles.

I further certify that no electronic communications were used to attract, locate, observe, or guide the hunter to such game; and that it was taken in full compliance with the local game laws or regulations of the state, province or territory.

Date   *February 1, 1970*   Hunter   *Al Firenze, Sr.*

OFFICIAL SCORING SYSTEM FOR NORTH AMERICAN BIG GAME TROPHIES

RECORDS OF NORTH AMERICAN
BIG GAME COMMITTEE

BOONE AND CROCKETT CLUB

Boone and Crockett Club
Records of North American Big Game Committee
c/o Carnegie Museum
4400 Forbes Ave. Pittsburgh, Pa. 15213

Minimum Score: 195:45 = 240

NON-TYPICAL MULE DEER

ABNORMAL	
Points Line E	
R	L
3 4/8	
3 6/8	
1 2/8	8
3 6/8	6 5/8
6 2/8	7 7/8
9 2/8	5 1/8
9 5/8	1 1/8
2 6/8	2
7 7/8	4
2 3/8	5 6/8
4 2/8	2 2/8
	3 1/8
1 2/8	
Totals 57 7/8	45 7/8
To E	103 6/8

DETAIL OF POINT MEASUREMENT

SEE OTHER SIDE FOR INSTRUCTIONS

	Supplementary Data R. / L.	Column 1	Column 2	Column 3	Column 4
	R. | L.	Spread	Right	Left	
A. Number of Points on Each Antler	18 | 15	Credit	Antler	Antler	Difference
B. Tip to Tip Spread	19 2/8				
C. Greatest Spread	40 2/8				
D. Inside Spread of MAIN BEAMS 22 1/8 Spread credit may equal but not exceed length of longer antler		22 1/8			
IF Inside Spread of Main Beams exceeds longer antler length, enter difference					
E. Total of Lengths of all Abnormal Points	103 6/8				
F. Length of Main Beam			22 5/8	21 3/8	1 2/8
G-1. Length of First Point, if present			3	3	
G-2. Length of Second Point			14 7/8	15 2/8	3/8
G-3. Length of Third Point, if present			10 5/8	11 7/8	1 2/8
G-4. Length of Fourth Point, if present			10	9 2/8	6/8
H-1. Circumference at Smallest Place Between Burr and First Point			4 6/8	5 1/8	3/8
H-2. Circumference at Smallest Place Between First and Second Points			5 1/8	4 7/8	2/8
H-3. Circumference at Smallest Place Between Main Beam and Third Point			5 3/8	4 6/8	5/8
H-4. Circumference at Smallest Place Between Second and Fourth Points			5	4 6/8	2/8
TOTALS	103 6/8	22 1/8	81 3/8	80 2/8	5 1/8

ADD	Column 1	22 1/8	Exact locality where killed North Kaibab, Arizona
	Column 2	81 3/8	Date killed 11-23-69 By whom killed Robert C. Rantz
	Column 3	80 2/8	Present owner Robert Rantz
	Total	183 6/8	Address Box 547, Williams, Arizona 86046
Subtract Column 4		5 1/8	Guide's Name and Address none
	Result	178 5/8	Remarks: (Mention any abnormalities)
Add Line E Total		103 6/8	
FINAL SCORE		282 3/8	

I certify that I have measured the above trophy on   *March 1*   19 *71*
at (address)   *Carnegie Museum*   City   *Pittsburgh*   State   *Pa.*
and that these measurements and data are, to the best of my knowledge and belief,
made in accordance with the instructions given.

Witness: *G. T. Church, Jr.*   Signature: *O. Uggen*

Boone and Crockett Official Measurer

Instructions

All measurements must be made with a flexible steel tape to the nearest one-eighth of an inch. Wherever it is necessary to change direction of measurement, mark a control point and swing tape at this point. To simplify addition, please enter fractional figures in *eighths*.

Official measurements cannot be taken for at least sixty days after the animal was killed. *Please submit photographs.*

Supplementary Data measurements indicate conformation of the trophy, and none of the figures in Lines A, B and C are to be included in the score. Evaluation of conformation is a matter of personal preference.

A. Number of Points on Each Antler. To be counted a point, a projection must be at least one inch long AND its length must exceed the length of its base. All points are measured from tip of point to nearest edge of beam as illustrated. Beam tip is counted as a point but not measured as a point.

B. Tip to Tip Spread measured between tips of Main Beams.

C. Greatest Spread measured between perpendiculars at right angles to the center line of the skull at widest part whether across beams or points.

D. Inside Spread of Main Beams measured at right angles to the center line of the skull at widest point between main beams. Enter this measurement again in "Spread Credit" column if it is less than or equal to the length of longer antler.

E. Total of Lengths of all Abnormal Points. Abnormal points are considered to be those nontypical in shape or location. It is very important, in scoring nontypical heads, to determine which points are to be classed as normal and which are not. To do this, study carefully the markings G–1, G–2, G–3 and G–4 on the diagram, which indicate the normal points. On the trophy to be scored, select the points which most closely correspond to these. *All others over one inch in length (See A, above) are considered abnormal.* Measure the exact length of each abnormal point, over the the outer curve, from the tip to the nearest edge of the beam or point from which it projects. Then add these lengths and enter the total in the space provided.

F. Length of Main Beam measured from lowest outside edge of burr over outer curve to the tip of the main beam. The point of beginning is that point on the burr where the center line along the outer curve of the beam intersects the burr.

G–1–2–3–4. Length of Normal Points. Normal points are the brow (or first) and the upper and lower forks as shown in illustration. They are measured from nearest edge of beam over outer curve to tip. To determine nearest edge (top edge) of beam, lay the tape along the outer curve of the beam so that the top edge of the tape coincides with the top edge of the beam on both sides of the point. Draw line along top edge of tape. This line will be base line from which point is measured.

H–1–2–3–4. Circumferences—If first point is missing, take H–1 and H–2 at smallest place between burr and second point. If third point is missing, take H–3 half way between the base and tip of second point. If the fourth point is missing take H–4 half way between the second point and tip of main beam.

Trophies Obtained Only by Fair Chase May Be Entered in Any Boone and Crockett Club Big Game Competition

To make use of the following methods shall be deemed UNFAIR CHASE and unsportsmanlike, and any trophy obtained by use of such means is disqualified from entry in any Boone and Crockett Club big game competition:

I. Spotting or herding game from the air, followed by landing in its vicinity for pursuit;

II. Herding or pursuing game with motor-powered vehicles;

III. Use of electronic communications for attracting, locating or observing game, or guiding the hunter to such game.

I certify that the trophy scored on this chart was not taken in UNFAIR CHASE as defined above by the Boone and Crockett Club.

I certify that it was not spotted or herded by guide or hunter from the air followed by landing in its vicinity for pursuit, nor herded or pursued on the ground by motor-powered vehicles.

I further certify that no electronic communications were used to attract, locate, observe, or guide the hunter to such game; and that it was taken in full compliance with the local game laws or regulations of the state, province or territory.

Date   *March 25, 1970*   Hunter   *Robert C. Rantz* add immeasurable depth and pleasure to any deer hunt.

When contracting a guide, make sure to get the process started well in advance of the hunting season. A year isn't really too soon. Word of mouth is still the most reliable recommendation, but in lieu of personal contact you can locate the names of reputable individuals through state fish and game agencies, local chambers of commerce, and the advertisements found in outdoor magazines.

If there is one piece of advice that covers all your prospecting for a guide, it is this: get it on paper. The cost to you, the services the guide will provide, where and when you will get picked up, the number of hunters in camp, the number of guides available to service them—any and every relevant detail you can think of.

It isn't so much a matter of an unscrupulous guide; these people are in a tiny minority and don't stay in business for long. Rather, it is you and your expectations. Speaking from some sad experiences as a licensed guide myself, I have seen too many people arrive at camp expecting things that aren't provided as part of the service. The list can run from sleeping bags to horses to cooks; some guides provide all these things, and many of them provide none of them. Guides are many things, but they are not clairvoyants. Unless you make perfectly clear what it is you expect, no one can tell you if he does or does not provide those goods and services. Then too, if you are told that those services are included in the package and you find that they are not, you have every reason to gripe—and the ammunition to back you up, right on paper.

Hunting Laws

Because laws are a management tool, and management problems and requirements vary with the habitat, laws, too, exhibit radical differences from state to state.

The legal limit of deer is a good case in point. Currently, in

Montana you can take two deer of either sex per year, sometimes three with a special permit. In New York you are allowed one deer, but unless you have a special permit the deer must be a buck.

There are, however, some generally employed laws that are universal. They are meant to enforce safety, common sense, and good sportsmanship.

• Licenses are required to hunt deer in all states. In most states you must first pass a hunter safety course before you can purchase a license. This is an excellent practice, one that I should personally like to see extended nationwide. I should also like to see course requirements expanded beyond their emphasis on safety alone. In most European countries, for example, neophyte hunters undergo extensive training in marksmanship, map reading, gun handling, game management, etiquette, and hunting techniques before being certified. This education engenders a spirit of sportsmanship and understanding that I find occasionally lacking in the American hunter.

• Hunting from a vehicle is generally illegal, including all forms of motorized transportation: trail bikes, snowmobiles, ATVs, and, of course, cars and pickups. In addition, shooting from or across a public road is against the law.

• Night hunting is illegal in all states, but just when "night" legally begins varies. Some states run their seasons a half hour before sunrise to a half hour after sundown. Others use sunrise and sundown as the limit. One other aspect of night "hunting" is sometimes illegal too: jacking or shining deer at night with a light. I personally get tremendous enjoyment out of watching deer at night, but because this is a favorite trick of illegal hunters, many fish and game departments prohibit the practice outright.

• Tags are required to be placed on the deer you shoot in many states. These tags are usually part and parcel of your license, and a tag must be affixed to the carcass immediately after the kill. Failure to tag an animal properly is the most common reason for having a carcass confiscated by game agents, so make sure that you observe all tagging laws in the state where you are hunting.

• Wasting deer meat is both unthinkable and illegal. When you kill an animal, you are expected to make full use of the carcass.

• Rifles for deer hunting must usually shoot a center-fire cartridge. The law is meant to eliminate the use of .22s, which commonly cripple more than they kill. For the same reason, long bows must generally have a pull in excess of thirty-five pounds.

• Other regulations are common enough to deserve mention, though not so common as to be universal. Carrying a loaded or uncased gun in a vehicle is usually illegal. Hunters must wear red or international orange (a common law in the Northern states, not so common in the South). "Baiting"—attracting deer to an area with food—is illegal. Using dogs to run deer is illegal (except in the South). Destroying all evidence of sex on a carcass is illegal. Selling deer meat is illegal, and shooting a deer for someone else is illegal.

Realize that the laws briefly outlined here are by no means a complete list of those employed by every state. They are only intended to point out some of the rules you are expected to obey afield—and perhaps thereby save you undeserved grief.

When you buy your license, make sure to ask for a synopsis of the fish and game laws and read them carefully. Only then will you be sure of all the regulations adopted and enforced in the state where you are hunting.

Weaponry

The kind of country you are hunting in should be the determining factor in your choice of a rifle rather than the species you are hunting or the size of your quarry. This is true of cali-

There is no one "all-around" deer rifle. Actions, calibers, and sights must be matched to your shooting preferences and, most important, to the terrain you are hunting.

Sil Strung

ber, the type of sight to use, and the action of the weapon.

A bullet amounts to a hunk of lead propelled by the explosion of a powder charge. The ratio of the weight of the lead to the volume of the powder contained in a particular cartridge is what gives each caliber its characteristic.

It is generally true that a relatively light bullet, pushed by a large charge of powder, will go fast, shoot flat, reach out for long distances, and have a lot of shocking power. Because of the relationship of all these characteristics, however, these fast-moving bullets are easily deflected. In a hotshot "varminter" load, the most radical of the "light lead lotsa powder" combinations, the bullet will literally explode if it strikes a wispy slip of grass. More typical hunting loads in this category will either explode or deflect wildly should they strike a twig.

On the other end of the spectrum, proportionately large bullets pushed around by smaller charges of powder will move slowly (2,000 to 2,500 feet per second), have a looping, lobbing

169

trajectory that makes them rather ineffective at ranges beyond 300 yards, and won't possess much shocking power. They will, however, plow through brush and remain true.

The far-reaching, flat-shooting loads, then, are the calibers to turn to when terrain indicates predominantly long shots. The brush-cutters are for close-in country. Simply by virtue of habits and habitat, the mule deer load would usually be the light, fast one, the whitetail load the heavy, slow one.

In terms of specific calibers, I feel that the .30-06 straddles the middle of the road. Although I don't think such a sporting arm exists, this comes close to being the "all-around caliber" because cartridges for the weapon are available in a wide variety of bullet weights and powder loads.

As a rule of thumb, weapons suitable for whitetail hunting are above .30 caliber: .30-30, .300, .30-06, .308, .35, and .358. There is no necessity for the use of a "magnum" cartridge either. You will seldom be confronted with a shot at a white-tail over 200 yards, so while a weapon that is accurate at 500 yards may be nice to brag about, it's superfluous. There is also the matter of shocking power: a far-reaching gun smashes a deer at close ranges, destroying tremendous amounts of meat.

In terms of specific calibers, I really like the .30-30 for extremely brushy situations when shots will most likely be under 50 yards. The caliber isn't overly powerful so it doesn't ruin meat, yet the bullet is heavy enough to remain true though its path may carry it through thumb-sized limbs.

For longer-range whitetail shooting, I like the .358, a caliber that is waning in popularity. The gun is something of a brute, but it's accurate up to 250 yards, will uproot any tree in its way, and doesn't blood-shoot meat. I also use this weapon for mule deer when I am still-hunting in relatively heavy timber.

Most arms manufacturers include all these top whitetail calibers in their product line, but a few makes and models are especially worthy of note.

The Winchester Model 94 is a lever-action carbine that has changed little over a history that has spanned eighty years. These guns have a feel and heft unique to the breed. They don't just shoulder: they slip into place, sights fall on target, and the weapon practically shoots itself. More than any other weapon I have ever shot, the 94 somehow fits both me and the occasion. And a lot of other hunters have felt the same way. The Model 94 and Marlin's Model 336, a comparable weapon, have probably downed more deer than all other makes and models combined.

Savage's Model 99 is another lever-action weapon I use and enjoy. It has a short stroke for fast loading and boasts of impressive accuracy. In addition, 99s are available in a wide choice of calibers from .243 to .308. Unfortunately, Savage discontinued the .358 caliber model I like so much.

Favored automatics for whitetail work include the durable Browning and Remington's Model 742 Woodsmaster. For extremely brushy situations, the 742 carbine comes with an 18½-inch barrel. If you are a fan of pumps, Remington also makes a rifle on that action, the 760 Gamemaster.

On the other end of the scale, calibers for mule deer and open-country shooting in excess of 200 yards generally fall below .30 caliber: .30-06, 7mm., .283, .270, .264, .257, .243, and .25-06.

Of these calibers, I favor four and lean heavily to one.

The .30-06 is a good choice because of its popularity. Shells can be bought anywhere, and are usually in good selection—something of a consideration when the nearest town larger than a general store is 100 miles from your camp.

But even in its lightest weights, the .30-06 cartridge lacks the zip of other calibers, limiting it somewhat as an effective weapon for long ranges.

The 7mm. mag is roughly the opposite: a monster of a far-reaching and powerful gun, accurate at phenomenal ranges. But if you hit an average-size muley with the weapon at close ranges

—under 200 yards—the animal evaporates. Well, maybe that's going a little too far, but you do destroy great amounts of meat.

Using copper-jacketed bullets doesn't help much either; it more or less reverses the problem. The bullet is driven so fast that it can go right through the animal, doing very little immediate damage.

In addition, most of the magnum calibers are punishing guns. Anyone who shoots them a lot runs the risk of developing an anticipatory flinch, for they wrack the whole body with recoil. Frankly, I don't think there's a need for all that power in deer hunting.

The .25-06 is a thoroughly delightful gun to shoot, with impressive ballistics: fast, flat, and far-reaching. Its popularity has grown immensely in the West, and many of my friends swear by its effectiveness, but I can't help having some nagging doubts.

The outer limits of its range are what bothers me. After 300 yards it loses a lot of poop and its small chunk of lead doesn't pack much energy. This means that shocking power drops off as well as the ability to kill cleanly, a matter of no small concern when deer could well offer a shot beyond that distance.

It's the .270 I personally favor as the ideal caliber for muleys. The cartridge is essentially a .30-06, necked down to fit a variety of bullet weights that offer the hunter quite a bit of latitude in matching his load to hunting conditions.

The .270 has plenty of power and speed, and the lead it shoots carries authority at long distances. But it isn't so powerful that its recoil punishes the hunter, or his table meat.

There is, of course, another factor in my favoritism: I have used a .270 a lot and know its capabilities and limitations. My familiarity with the caliber also includes some nostalgic memories of old friends and horse camps in the backcountry, and burly bucks etched against a plains sky. You can't totally divorce a gun from personality, and I guess that's one of the reasons why the "right" weapon will always be a matter of debate equal to religion and politics.

Winchester's Model 94 has a noble history, an impressive record, and a heft and feel that suit the deer hunter and his sport.

The Savage 99 is another lever action well suited to brushy terrain. Modern in visual and internal design, this sporting arm is easily 'scoped, should that be your sighting persuasion.

Pumps are ever-popular actions for woodland work; at the top of the poll is Remington's short-barreled "gamemaster," available in .30-06 and .308 caliber.

Browning's automatic is an impressive weapon with a record of bolt-action-type accuracy. It is available in a wide variety of calibers. It is this action, in .30-06 caliber, that I personally feel comes closest to hitting the "all-around weapon" mark (though I don't think an "all-around weapon" exists).

Actions include bolt, lever, pump, and automatic. Because of the sudden snap-shot nature of hunting deer in brushy country, the bolt action is the least desirable for this situation. Not only is it the slowest to reload, but the manual activity involved in rechambering a shell usually causes you to momentarily lose your target in your sights.

I also find this a problem with lever actions. I don't think it's as acute as with a bolt, but working the lever isn't exactly a smooth operation, and the few seconds it takes to line up once more on a bounding, dodging whitetail could well cost you your deer.

Pump actions, in the hands of an expert, are the fastest of all to reload. They are also smooth to work, and keep you on target.

Personally, I favor the autos in the woodlands. I'm not one of those "experts" at reloading a pump, and I find being able to squeeze off four fast shots with no more effort than a twitch of my trigger a real advantage.

For long-range shooting, bolt actions are perfectly acceptable. They boast foolproof operation and excellent accuracy, and because your target will be in relatively open terrain, the speed of an auto-loader or pump isn't of paramount importance.

When hunting muleys out West, don't be surprised, however, if you find lever actions quite popular with the locals. But I think their predominance is a matter of habit rather than any special recommendation for operation or accuracy. The lever action is the old, standard saddle carbine, used by cavalry and cowboy alike. The use of these guns is practically tradition in the West, like cowboy hats and boots, and every ranch house isn't a home unless it has at least one such rifle by the door, usually a .30-30.

Southpaws, one of which I happen to be, do have some problems with bolt-action guns since they have to reach across scope and sight to manipulate the bolt. Left-handed bolt-action rifles are available from several major manufacturers. You might also consider an automatic. At one time autos had a reputation for poor accuracy at long ranges, but the manufacturer of mine, Browning, points with pride to some pretty impressive proofs of accuracy. Three years' personal experience also tends to support their claims; I have made some real bragging shots with the weapon.

For specific recommendations, Savage's Model 110 bolt action is both moderately priced and well designed. The trigger is crisp, the heft pleasant and well balanced, and the action smooth. This is one of the bolt actions that are available in left-handed models. Another rifle I am learning to love is Remington's Model 700. My wife shoots this one in 6mm. magnum, and it is her personal favorite. She has made some shots that have shamed me, to back up her preference.

As with Winchester's Model 94, there is something about their bolt-action Model 70 that's a classic. Gun buffs generally agree that the quality of the weapon dropped off after 1964, but the word now is that the old Model 70, with a few design changes, is back. I welcome it wholeheartedly. Now if they will just make a left-handed model. . . .

Sights fall into three categories: open, peep and scope. For most hunting situations, I have found the peep the poorest choice. First, for real accuracy, a tiny aperture is the best. However, these pinpoint inserts totally blank out in poor light. It is even difficult to make out a target when you are standing in the sun and your deer is in the shade.

These small apertures on a peep are usually removable, however, leaving a larger hole through which to sight. Although they don't gray out in half light, they are not nearly so accurate as the pinhole and I have seen them clog up regularly. Your gun slides off a resting spot on a tree . . . or you walk through thick brush . . . or encounter a snowstorm, and the hole picks up dirt, or bark, or snow. Usually, you don't realize it until a deer

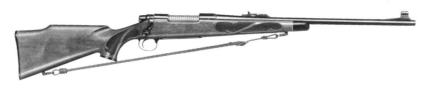

Remington's Model 700 BDL is light, quick, and smooth. I am particularly impressed by its trigger—crisp, but not so crisp that you can anticipate the hammer fall. It is a sure cure for one of a shooter's accuracy problems: flinching.

Savage's 110 line of bolt-action rifles includes a wide variety of calibers, and substantial quality when stacked up against their low, low price. What is more, they are available in left-handed actions, welcome news to any southpaw.

"Model 70" is a calling card that long-range shooters dote on. Because quality, performance, and results were so impressive before 1964, this vintage of Winchester's famous rifle commands top dollar today— often more than the original purchase price. But before you go looking for old "70s," check the new ones out. Experts advise me that they have gone back to the pre-'64 standards and design, news that will warm the heart of any tack driver.

bounds off, and then you have neither the time nor the deliberate patience to clear your sight.

It also takes a bit longer to pick up your target in a peep. Open sights can be used shotgun-style, and your sights sort of melt into position. Because a peep requires you to get your target inside a circle, and part of that circle is bound to block a clear view, a lot more fidgeting and alignment and time are required to get on target.

Finally, because of their design and position on a rifle, they are an open invitation to hard knocks that alter accuracy. I have also seen the things completely knocked off.

True, the peep is more accurate than open sights, but its disadvantages in brush and the tremendous advantages offered by scopes relegate it to third place in my scheme of values and valuables afield.

Open sights are the wisest choice for extremely brushy terrain. They line up fast and at close ranges provide more than enough accuracy. When shots are commonly 50 yards and closer, a scope of any magnification at all registers too large an image; instead of an animal, you will just see hair.

At ranges of 75 yards and beyond, I like a scope. It affords pinpoint accuracy and has light-gathering powers that give you something of a sighting edge at dawn and dusk.

I do not, however, favor great magnifications; a 2- or 2½-power scope is all that is needed for ranges up to 200 yards. Beyond that, a 4-power is plenty. Not only do high magnifications create too large an image; they zero in on such a relatively small piece of scenery that it is often difficult to locate your target immediately.

A recent development in hunting optics is a wide-angle scope. I have tried out this scope, though not afield, and it seems to help the "finding" problem immensely. One piece of gadgetry that I don't recommend for deer hunting is the variable or adjustable scope. This is a scope that can be cranked up or down to magnifications that run from 2½- to 10-power. It sounds good in theory, but creates problems in practice.

Weight is one problem; no matter how you get to the hunting grounds, you are going to be doing some walking, and this big tube adds as much as 5 pounds to the weight of your rifle. This weight also has a lot to do with the feel and balance of your weapon, and for me it has been a negative influence. Finally, I have seen these scopes foul up too many shots. Usually, a hunter will keep them on a high setting for glassing distant slopes. When a deer jumps up within 200 yards and the guy tries to sight in on him, he can't find the animal; the field of vision is too narrow. He has to lower his rifle, crank the scope back down to a reasonable setting, then reshoulder his weapon. In that period of time, the deer, or at least the best shot of the day, can easily be gone.

I favor light cross hairs in a scope over dots or command posts. While their lines may fade in the glimmer of dawn and dusk, their pinpoint precision is often needed to place a long shot. Another feature I like incorporated into a scope is a range finder. If you are not capable of judging distances, learn to use one of these and you will really improve accuracy.

Mounts for scopes come in several styles: swing-away, over-bore, offset, and solid. I prefer a solid mount for my muley weapon, just because it is what they say it is: solid.

Climbing around rock, walking in snow, or just bouncing around in a pickup truck are all activities that are bound to produce some heavy shocks, and without a solid mount your scope can easily be thrown out of accuracy.

For whitetail hunting and the possibility of thick brush, you might, however, consider an overbore scope mount. This gives you the latitude to shoot through a scope or open sights. The mount is essentially an open O, with the scope on top. To see your open sights, just drop down from the reticule and look through the O.

• A single-point scope doesn't magnify any image, but rather projects onto your target a dot that shows where the bullet will hit. It is the fastest to use of all the sights I have tried, and works beautifully in poor light conditions. It does, however, take some getting used to. I recently had a very respectable six-point go roaring by my stand and became so totally flabbergasted with the unfamiliar device that I never took a shot. I kept closing one eye from force of habit, when the model I have requires that both eyes be kept open.

Shotguns are occasionally used in conjunction with hunting white-tailed deer. In some states, deer populations and human populations are in such close proximity that the 2- or 3-mile carry of a rifle bullet is potentially dangerous. In this situation, hunters are required by law to use a shotgun, usually loaded with a slug.

These projectiles are usually themselves rifled, so that they will get some spin—and resulting accuracy—out of the smooth bore of a shotgun. Slugs are rather accurate up to 80 or 100 yards, but then their accuracy drops sharply.

In the Southern states, dense forests often dictate the wisdom of a shotgun loaded with buckshot. Shots at deer in these thick swamps and forests seldom exceed 30 yards, and they are often taken right through the branches of a tree. One slug or bullet could easily become lodged in a tree or deflect wild of its target. Buckshot sprays the area with flying lead, assuring that at least some of the load will reach its destination.

Buckshot comes in five sizes: No. 4 buck, No. 2 buck, buck, 0 buck, and 00 buck. No. 4 buck is roughly the size of a .22 bullet, and 00 buck about half the size of a marble. Thirty pellets of No. 4 buck are contained in a 12-gauge cartridge, and 9 pellets of 00 buck.

I flatly favor 00 buck for all situations where buckshot is used. First, buckshot is notoriously short-range stuff, and its killing power is further reduced as you use smaller and smaller shot.

Tied to range is penetration: No. 4 buck simply won't go as deeply and kill as cleanly as 00, and, of course, the more pellets you sling around, the more meat you will tear up.

For both buckshot and slugs, 12-gauge is the favorite. A 12-gauge is the largest of the common gauges, so its load packs plenty of punch. It is also the most popular, so both slugs and buckshot are easy shells to find in local stores. This isn't the case with other gauges.

When it comes to the weapons themselves, short, 26-inch barrels are the best. A longer barrel doesn't give you any greater reach, and a long gun is far more likely to collide with a twig or a tree as you swing on a running target. A full choke is preferred for buckshot, an open choke for slugs.

Favored actions for deer shotguns are pumps and automatics. Both hold between three and five shells, are fast-loading, and remain on target during the rechambering process. Automatics are far and away the favorite of most hunters, and many manufacturers offer a "deer special" particularly designed for this type of hunting in their lines of shotguns.

Sights on guns used for buckshot don't make much sense. With a maximum range of 50 yards and nine bullets careening through the air, accuracy isn't going to be markedly increased by pinpoint sighting.

On a slug gun, sights aren't a bad idea. The best of the slugs are relatively accurate up to 100 yards, so the extra precision a sight offers can be a help. I don't, however, recommend anything beyond garden-variety open sights.

Knives

I see an awful lot of deer hunters with knives that look almost comic. Heavy, huge, and wicked-looking, they are just a shade too small to chop trees and far too big to either skin or gut a deer. A deer hunter should have two knives: one for cutting and gutting and the other for skinning. The cutting knife should be light and short-bladed. I see no reason for a blade longer than 4½ inches. The blade design should incorporate a perfectly flat back and a point that is in line with the back of the knife or, better yet, slightly turned down.

My reasons for recommending this design are all tied in with the gutting process. A long-bladed knife with a needle-sharp turned-up point is bound to puncture the viscera, thus tainting the meat. Conversely, a short blade with a rounded point tends to separate the viscera from the stomach wall as it moves along.

Further, there is no need for a larger knife to do the other cutting jobs a deer hunter will face afield. Slicing through the windpipe, ribs, and pelvic bone is easily accomplished with this design.

Skinning knives should also have a short blade; 5 inches is plenty. Like gutting knives, they should have a turned-down point to prevent them from puncturing hide or flesh as they slice between the two.

A skinning knife should, however, have a comparatively broad blade—1 to 1½ inches wide—with the tip area rounded to the point of exaggeration and broader than the knife blade at the hilt.

This is desirable because it is the tip area that does most of the slicing, probing under the skin, then cutting it free with a circular sweep of the wrist. The blade should be broad for leverage; twisted sideways, it will help peel back the hide.

An honest skinning knife is hard to come by these days. I know of only one manufacturer that makes them: Buck Knives Inc., P.O. Box 126, El Cajon, California 92022. The knives are available in stores and by mail order for around $15.

I have some opinions about knife steel as well as design. Manufacturers go to great lengths promoting the toughness of their high-carbon steel knives—devices that can slice through carriage bolts and skewer silver dollars like so much shish kebab.

The deer hunter needs two knives: one for gutting and one for skinning. Neither should be overly large, and both work best if they have a slightly turned-down point.

I have owned some of these knives and have no use for them. They take forever to get a razor edge and then don't hold it long. It's that edge that I demand for cutting. I much prefer a milder, low-carbon steel for my knife blades. They don't hold a razor edge any longer than knives of harder steel do, but they will take that edge with a few strokes of a stone and leather, both of which are part of my sheath.

Knife sharpening requires the use of a two-gritted stone and leather. If you have a very dull knife, begin with the coarsest grit.

Lay the knife flat on its side, then raise it on its cutting edge so that the flat of the knife barely clears the stone. The angle will be between 15 and 25 degrees, depending on the thickness of the blade.

Move the cutting edge into the grit in a smooth half circle

so that all parts of the edge, especially the rounded tip area, come in contact with the stone. Turn the knife over and repeat the process.

Continue this until you create an edge, turning the knife over and over for each stroke to ensure an even bevel on each side of the blade. On this coarse grit, you can bear down quite hard.

Once you have an edge you can feel, move on to the fine grit, repeating the process described above. Begin by bearing down on each stroke, then gradually decrease the pressure. The final strokes should be featherlight.

Again using the fine grit, sharpen some more, but this time add oil or water to the surface of the stone. This lubricates the abrasives so that they don't wear the steel so rapidly and, in turn, creates an even finer edge. Finish with featherlight strokes.

Leather stropping is the final process. An old razor strop is the best device to use, though any strip of well-oiled leather will do the job. In the field I use my belt, boot, or knife sheath.

Strop the knife away from the cutting edge this time. If you have done a good job on the stone, about eight strops in either direction should give you a gleaming edge you can literally shave with.

That keen edge should last for the gutting of one deer, assuming that you don't use your knife for throwing, whittling, opening tin cans, or cutting carriage bolts. Because you have established an acute bevel, you should be able to hone another razor edge after about a minute with an oiled stone and leather strop. Realize, however, that with each new razor edge you are wearing down that fine bevel, and will have to regrind it after long use. I find that I have to work my knife down about every six months, but it sees a lot of service.

This same type of bevel is perfectly acceptable on an ax used for cutting wood. A splitting ax, on the other hand, should have a less acute bevel, since its broad "V" produces a wedging effect, wrenching the wood apart. Understandably, a wedging bevel will hold an edge a lot longer than a cutting bevel, and therein lies the secret to the claim of many knife makers that their product will "hold an edge forever."

Between the hard steel they use and the type of edge they put on a knife, they are quite right. They neglect to mention, however, that their product doesn't cut worth a damn.

Deer Hunting with Bow and Arrow

A bow and arrow offers some unique opportunities in terms of deer hunting that simply aren't available to the man who hunts only with a gun. From a purely practical standpoint, bow hunters are commonly granted a special season before the regular gun season opens, and sometimes another special season after it closes. By being a bow hunter, you can then enjoy hunting for three, sometimes four, months out of the year. Archers also usually enjoy an either-sex season and are often the exclusive participants in "special hunts" conducted on military bases, game management preserves, and industrial properties. Still another bonus occurs in bag limits: many states allow a hunter to take one deer with a bow, and a second with a gun during the regular season.

Aesthetically speaking, archery is truly a primitive hunting method, one that both suggests and evokes a feeling of the primal relationship between hunter and hunted that has existed since man first learned to use rocks and sticks as weapons.

Hunting with a gun is certainly legitimate and enjoyable, but in that weapon I sometimes see an undesirable intermediary— a machine of man that has a questionable place between the deer and me.

Bows, too, I suppose, could be called "a machine of man," but they are not so cold and metallic or so damnably efficient. In bow hunting, there are no long, impartial shots, no booming guns or noisy drives to shatter the silence of the woods. It's an

Hunting deer with a bow and arrow is both demanding and difficult. Getting a shot like this requires skill, stealth, and infinite patience.

Michigan Department of Natural Resources

exercise in stealth involving you, the deer, and the forest, with ranges measured in feet, not hundreds of yards. Patience, knowledge, and skill are prerequisites to success, but not guarantees. Luck is a valuable ally.

If it sounds as if I'm a bow-hunting fan, you are right. If it sounds as if it's a demanding sport, you are right on that count too.

Equipment is rather basic, reflecting the relative simplicity of the sport. Modern hunting bows fall into two categories: the recurve and the compound bow.

The recurve bow has a gull-wing design, with a flowing curve that extends out from the center, and curves back against itself near each bow tip. The recurve design propels an arrow faster than an equivalent-weight longbow, and it does this job with less total length. This matter of bow length is rather important when hunting; overly long bows get hung up on brush as you walk, or when you kneel, stretch, or bend to get a clear shot around an obstruction.

Compound bows are so new and varied that many states have not legalized them. A system of pulleys and stout limbs that appear most unbowlike, they look like some medieval war machine. Their efficiency, however, can't be put down. At a fifty-pound pull of the archer's arm, they deliver an arrow with seventy-five pounds' worth of thrust. They are also considerably shorter than a recurve bow, making for a few important edges there.

Resistance to change is probably why I favor the recurve. There is also the matter of machinery. But I am sure that people said the same thing about the recurve when it was first introduced some twenty years ago.

Bows are measured in pounds. When you draw back on the bowstring, pressure is exerted on your fingers. At full draw, the amount of pressure exerted is the bow's rating. Hunting bows are never less than thirty-five pounds and commonly more. Standard hunting weights run forty-five to fifty-five pounds.

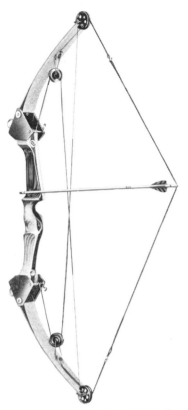

Allen Archery Company

Through a system of pulleys, the compound bow delivers a light, short arrow at greater thrust and speed than an equivalent-weight recurve.

The graceful recurve is the most popular hunting bow in America. Construction is usually a laminate of wood and fiber glass.

Browning

The matter of draw deserves discussion too. Because of individual differences in build and arm length, archers have different draw lengths—essentially the distance from the bow to the bowstring when the bow is comfortably flexed. Standard draw is 28 inches, but arrows are available in 26- and 30-inch draws.

Arrows are best when they are either aluminum or fiber glass.

Both these materials make for a perfectly straight and true shaft and won't warp. Aluminum arrows are the most accurate, but they won't stand up as well as fiber glass.

Arrows have to be balanced with your bow, both in terms of their length (to correspond to your draw), and a thing called spine weight. Spine weight is matched to the pull of your bow and is an indication of the relative stiffness of the arrow shaft. An overly limber shaft, shot from a too powerful bow, will severely bend in air from the force of inertia, which in turn affects accuracy. It can also splinter, causing injury.

One feature I would recommend in any arrows you buy is removable heads. That way you can use the same shafts for target practice and hunting; just unscrew your field heads and replace them with broadheads. The merits associated with this practice are a matter of familiarity; even the best shafts exhibit subtle differences, and when you stick with one set for both practice and hunting, you come to know them.

Another way to achieve this all-important familiarity is to purchase "split packs" of arrows. These amount to a dozen arrows of identical manufacture, six with hunting heads, six with field heads.

A modern quiver that holds arrows in firm place to keep them from rattling is essential. A back quiver is the poorest choice. Even one designed to rest in line with your neck will get hung up in brush when you have to bend low. A side quiver that you wear on your hip is better, but it occasionally gets tangled too. I favor the bow quiver, a device that is anchored to your bow and holds between three and five shafts parallel to the bow's limbs. Since the arrows are essentially part of your bow, all you have to worry about is getting it through thick brush.

Armguards and finger guards are necessary for target practice to keep both appendages from being worn out by the snapping bowstring. I don't care to wear finger guards while hunting;

you don't get enough shots to bother your fingertips. Armguards, however, are a good idea afield. They keep loose clothing from getting tangled in the snapping bowstring and throwing your accuracy askew.

Brush buttons—small rubber buttons that slide over your bowstring and rest where string joins limb—will prevent a lot of cussing and frustration. Without them, brush will constantly become wedged between your string and the end of the bow. Brush buttons also silence the twang of a snapped string; often deer will hear that twang and bolt, dodging the arrow before it reaches them. Their reactions are just that finely keened.

Total camouflage is another essential to success: hat, clothing, boots, right down to greasepaint on your hands, face, and ears. If you can't find camouflage greasepaint, use burnt cork.

The necessity for long hours of target practice is debatable. You of course have to be familiar with your weapon, but competition-level arrow spitting at 50 yards isn't a prerequisite to bow hunting. Past surveys have indicated that hunting ability is far more central to success than pinpoint accuracy.

The type of accuracy required to score is best achieved by learning to be consistent. There are many variables involved in shooting a bow—far more than in a rifle—so the more variables you can correct, the more accurate your shot will be.

For example, when fitting the arrow to the bowstring (called nocking the arrow), you will eliminate one of those variables if you will nock at precisely the same point each time. There is also an optimum spot for nocking, a point on the string $\frac{1}{8}$ to $\frac{1}{4}$ inch above the arrow rest on the bow shaft. To achieve this consistency and precise positioning, a small button or roll of tape is usually attached to the string. By snugging the arrow up to the button, you are assured of the same nocking point every time.

Draw is another factor in accuracy. For predictable results, you should pull the string the same distance for each shot. This area of consistency is commonly achieved by an "anchor point," a place on your face you first touch with your drawing hand before releasing the arrow. The most common anchor technique is to touch the corner of your mouth with the string.

Bow sights are another shortcut to accuracy. These devices are either clamped or taped to the bow next to the arrow rest. The best bow sights have three or four "sight beads" or "pointers" arranged vertically along the bow face and marked for yardage: 20, 30, 40, and so forth. After a bow is correctly sighted in, you can then line up the sight bead that corresponds to the estimated yardage from your deer, and you will be automatically on target with the right elevation and lateral correction.

Some manufacturers also incorporate "range finders" into their sights. A range finder usually amounts to a sighting window with lines or wires running at right angles to your bow. The distances between the lines are irregular, designed to frame a portion of an animal's anatomy at different yardages. When a sighted animal fits between the lines marked "30," he is 30 yards away. Put the sighting bead marked "30" on his chest, and if your draw and release are smooth, you should connect.

Bow sights aren't a prerequisite to accuracy, however. Many able archers don't use them. But without a sight, you will have to develop some aiming system. Ken Yaeger, outdoor writer and incurable bow hunter, taught me the following:

Sight a bow as you would a rifle. The string should be drawn back so it centers squarely in front of your aiming eye. That is your rear sight. The tip of the drawn arrow is your front sight. Line the two up and you have lateral correction.

Judging distances is another factor in the long list of archery variables. Obviously, you have to hold higher for a 30-yard shot than for a 10-yard shot.

One way you can learn to judge distances is by looking at the bases of trees. Their sizes and shapes are hardly uniform, so

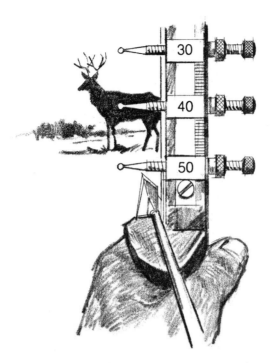

Bow sights provide a consistent point of aim and increase accuracy.

when you can pick out a young hickory, decide that it's 25 yards away, and pace off between 23 and 27 yards from you to it, you are getting someplace.

Once you get that distance judging down, you are also going to have to learn how much elevation you need to be accurate at that distance. A system that has worked reasonably well for me is to raise my aim half the depth of the deer's body for every 10 yards between me and my target.

For example, at 10 yards I hold right on for the center of the body. At 20, I shoot for the back. At 30, I hold between 12 and 18 inches above the back, and so forth.

Because of the importance of knowing ranges, I also strongly favor a life-size paper or full-bodied replica of a deer for practice. It's a quick and natural way to learn how big a deer looks at 10, 20, or 40 yards. Another plus in using a facsimile of the animal is that you learn to shoot for a specific spot rather than the whole animal. This is a mistake often made by beginning archers, and they fail to connect with a killing shot as a result.

Exactly how proficient you should be with a bow before venturing afield is a question of some debate. The popular consensus is heavy on accuracy at long ranges—40 yards and beyond. But speaking from personal experience, I have gotten most of my shots well under that range: 20 to 25 yards is about average, so I feel being able to place arrows in an 8-inch circle at that distance is an able beginning.

However accurate you may or may not be with a bow, though, never lose sight of the fact that hunting ability is the paramount factor in success. You may be able to skewer a pie plate at 40 yards, but unless you can get that close to a deer unnoticed, that skill will do you little good.

Although a hunting arrow in flight possesses a surprising amount of energy, arrows have no shocking power like the explosive smash of a bullet. They kill by creating a massive hemorrhage—by cutting through flesh and arteries, so that the deer bleeds to death.

This is the reason for the wicked-looking designs of hunting broadheads, with razor inserts, spirals, and crisscrossed blades. It's also the reason why these heads must be kept razor-sharp: a dull arrowhead just means a wounded deer unless you are lucky and hit him in the heart, and even then the arrow may not be sharp enough to drive home.

Since massive bleeding is paramount to a quick, effective kill, it is necessary to aim only for those spots that will produce this result.

Like gun hunting, the lung area is the most sensible because of its size and vulnerability. Get used to aiming right behind the shoulder, a little bit lower than midway down the animal's side. Another possible shot at this area would be straight down:

if you are in a tree stand and a deer walks under you, aim slightly to the left or right of the center of the deer's back, just behind his shoulders.

Deer have, of course, been killed by shots that hit in other areas. A friend of mine killed a beautiful eight-point whitetail when he hit him in the lower hind leg! But he, and other hunters who have made a kill in areas other than the lungs, were lucky enough to sever an artery, or smash through the backbone to cut the spinal cord.

Except for that unusual spinal-cord shot, a deer struck with an arrow can be expected to run. How far it will run is a matter of the seriousness of the wound; a lung shot should drop an animal within 100 yards, but I have heard hunters tell of hard-hit deer who ran much further.

The important thing is to ascertain whether or not a "missed" deer was hit. Generally, if you can't find your arrow, you should assume that you connected. Even if you do find your arrow, check the shaft for blood. Quite often, an arrow will pass right through a deer.

If you think you made a hit, tracking can be quite difficult, since much of the deer's bleeding can be internal. Go immediately to the spot where you last saw the deer and start searching for blood spots. You will probably have to get down on your hands and knees and examine the trail leaf by leaf. It also pays to leave something at that spot on the trail, so you can reorient yourself should you get turned around in your search.

Although I favor an immediate follow-up when I have hit a deer with a bullet, I don't recommend immediately following a blood trail when you have connected with an arrow. Since hemorrhage is invariably the cause of death, you are better off to give it time to occur. Wait a minimum of fifteen minutes before striking the trail. If you jump the animal, again wait at least fifteen minutes before looking some more.

Although this difficulty in tracking would seem to support

Deer Hunting

one of the most frequent criticisms of bow hunting—that it results in too many wounded but not harvested deer—this isn't the case. Surprisingly enough, recent studies completed in Wisconsin and New York indicate that cripple loss from bow hunters is on a proportional par with that from gun hunters.

Archery is primarily a sport that centers in on the whitetail, because the dense cover this deer frequents affords an opportunity to slip within a 10- to 30-yard range of a bowshot. Still-hunting is the most absorbing way to hunt with a bow, but tree stands account for the most kills.

Mule deer can be hunted with a bow, but I have never found them holed up in thick enough timber to allow a bow hunter to get within range. The one mule deer I have shot with a bow was taken from a blind located along a trail used by deer feeding in a hayfield.

Should you down a deer you think rates as a trophy, contact the archers' trophy club, the Pope and Young Club, since archers have their own system of measurement. Inquiries may be made to Richard L. Mauch, P.O. Box J, Bassett, Nebraska 68714.

Clothing

Clothing for the deer hunter performs two functions: safety and warmth.

In terms of safety, red is the traditional color; however, recent tests have indicated that under poor light conditions this color can appear brown to some individuals—a rather unhealthful state of affairs when the woods are full of people looking for brown deer.

Conversely, researchers have determined that there is one color that can be mistaken for no other. International orange, day-glo orange, reflective orange—it goes by many names, and indeed is a recognizable shade that appears nowhere in nature. What is more, it seems to have light-gathering qualities. In the near-darkness of predawn and postdusk, a man wearing an orange vest disappears, but his vest stands out bright and ghostlike, much like the ridiculous bra and girdle ads endured on TV.

While there is no question about the safety of this color—and the real need to be recognized immediately by other hunters —I do think it puts you at a disadvantage with the deer.

I have heard time and again the claim that deer can't see color, yet personal experience continues to point up indications that they can. Bow hunting alone supports this; wearing camouflage, I have gotten close enough to some deer to wipe their noses; this has never happened during the gun season when I always wear red, unless, of course, I am thoroughly concealed in a blind.

The solution to this problem is a difficult one, if there is a solution at all. While I am familiar with the dynamics of deer vis-à-vis human vision, I can't help wondering if a camouflage pattern imposed on an orange background may not be the answer. To date, I know of no manufacturer offering this product, so there is some food for thought for someone who might like to make a million bucks.

Choosing clothing that will keep you warm is a less thorny issue. In general, you are wise to overdress rather than underdress. You can always open a collar or crack a zipper when you are too warm, but there is not much you can do when biting cold starts eating through to body and bone toward sundown —except shiver a lot.

When selecting your clothing, remember that several layers of light clothing will keep you warmer than one heavy jacket. For extremely cold temperatures, cotton underwear to absorb perspiration, then Dacron-quilted underwear over that, makes for extremely warm foundation garments. Sweaters, so long as they are covered by some sort of windbreaker, are quite efficient, since they trap a lot of air and it is dead air that keeps you warm.

On the whole, wool is the best all-around material for the

hunter for both inner and outer wear. Though it is a bit heavier than the other two logical alternatives—synthetic fiber and down insulation—neither of these materials will keep you warm when you are wet. Wool will. Wool is also the most silent material. Virtually any other fiber, natural or synthetic, will squeak, slap, swish, or crackle as you walk through the woods.

Footwear for warm weather should be light. I favor the low-cut hiking boots so popular with mountain climbers and back-packers. They are far cooler and less heavy than high-top boots. One drawback to this style is that seeds and chaff can get around your ankle and itch you into insanity. But you can eliminate that possibility by buying and wearing canvas uppers, available in most stores that cater to backpackers, over the boottop.

In cold and inclement weather, high-top boots are best. Choose a boot with a square, rather high heel if you will be around snow. Flat heel-to-toe profiles on the sole of boots will turn them into skis when you are going downhill.

For tread design, I personally favor a shallow corrugation rather than heavy lugs that look as if they have been lifted from a snow tire. While they appear to have the inherent grip of hobnails, these big lugs get easily clogged with mud and wet snow, and you again end up with skis.

Leather is still the superior performer for boot construction. It is the only material tough enough to take a hard beating afield, porous enough to allow transfer of perspiration, yet impervious to serious leakage of rain or snow.

Signs of quality in leather construction are all centered around seaming. Seams which are numerous and exposed generally indicate an inferior boot. Seams are the most likely place for water to enter, and a potential weak spot; stitching can easily become frayed and broken from the normal cuts and abrasions that are part of a day spent walking in the woods.

As with any new footwear, break your boots in thoroughly before putting in a full day of wearing them. The best way I have found to do this is to wear them while puttering around the house for a week or so previous to their first long walk.

And while we are on the subject of feet, some mention of socks may be in order. The most agreeable arrangement I have yet to find is the new "wick-dry" socks worn inside a heavy pair of wool socks. The wool provides insulation and warmth, and the wick-dry socks, as the manufacturers claim, do seem to take the moisture of perspiration away from your skin. And as any woodlands slogger knows, it is dampness that is usually the main cause of cold feet.

5

Carcass Care

IN MY SYSTEM OF VALUES, what you do with a deer after it is dead defines you as a hunter more than the collective weight of all the skills, knowledge, and effort required to kill the animal in the first place.

Part of this philosophy is purely romantic, and therefore hard to define, but maybe a few blanket Indians would still understand. Because I have killed the animal, I owe it, or its spirit, the simple respect of not wasting this gift. And there is no greater waste than spoiled meat.

Memories play a part in it too. A hunting trip lasts only a short time, but the meat of the deer and its quality will provide you not only with food for thought but food for your table throughout the year.

Finally the pragmatist comes through. Correctly treated deer meat tastes damn good—better than beef. Its texture and grain are as fine as thread and tender as veal, the meat is lean and of delicate flavor, and it is not laced and loaded with chemicals to make it sterile, fat, happy, or more palatable.

And while we are on the subject of flavor, so-called "gaminess" as an inherent quality of any carcass of deer meat is a myth. As an act of mercy, I have killed deer wounded by other hunters hours before and sick with fever and I have found the food perfectly fit for the table. I have also downed a buck in rut, with a distended neck as big as a tree trunk, smelling strongly of the perfume of musk and battle madness. He reminded me of an old billy goat before he was butchered. But when the meat was placed on the table, next to another bowl of beef chunks, for a backyard shish kebab, everyone going back for seconds took the deer.

The care that results in this kind of good-tasting meat begins the moment the animal hits the ground. First, make sure that the deer is dead. Approaching from the rear hindquarter, prod the deer with your rifle barrel. If there is no sign of life, move toward the head. If the eyes are closed, the deer may still be alive; if they are open and glassy, touch the eyes with the muzzle of your rifle. Should they remain unblinking, you can be virtually sure that the deer is dead, but you should still be cautious. More than one hunter has been severely kicked or gored by a "dead" deer.

In preparation for the gutting process, stand to the side and work the hind legs. Occasionally muscle spasms will cause them to kick out even though the animal has expired, and moving the legs by hand will trigger that reaction if it is going to occur.

Next, lay the deer squarely on the middle of its back. If you have a friend handy, he can hold the animal in this position. If no one is around, you will have to shore up the carcass with rocks or logs. Try to have the carcass as level as possible. If you are on a steep hill, lay the animal at right angles to the fall line.

Begin entry into the body cavity by grasping a hank of hair from the center-belly, 4 to 5 inches above the genital area. Pull the hair straight up. This pulls skin and muscle away from the viscera, so that the first incision won't puncture the stomach or intestine.

Insert the knife into the upraised skin gently, teasing a larger and larger incision as you go. You will have to slice through the skin proper, then several layers of meaty muscle tissue, before you reach the inner cavity.

Once you have punctured the body cavity, the major task at hand is to open it further without slicing into organs or getting hair on the meat. Deer belly hair is often laced with musk or urine and can taint a silver-dollar-sized area of meat.

To do this, guide your knife with index and middle finger in a V position. Point the edge of the knife away from the crotch of your fingers, and move your hand forward as you cut. Use your fingers, inside the carcass, to keep the viscera separated from the stomach wall.

Essentially, this operation has you cutting from the inside out, so that very little hair is cut loose by the knife.

As you approach the heart/lung area, you will hit the ribs. You can continue cutting through the ribs with your knife if you will move the blade slightly (about 2 inches) to the left or right of the center-chest area. Cutting through the ribs will be more difficult than in the stomach area, but you can bring both hands to bear on the knife handle since the organs in the chest won't taint meat even if you do cut into them.

If you have a trophy you want to mount, end the cut at a point even with the two front legs. If you are interested only in meat, continue the cut right up to the throat area. The more you expose the carcass to air, the quicker it will cool. That is one of the tricks to good-tasting meat.

Cut the windpipe from the outside. You will be able to feel it, round and hard and a bit like a vacuum-cleaner hose, all along the deer's throat. Stick the point of the knife behind it, push it through the hide up to the hilt, and cut up and out in one clean stroke. On a trophy animal, the windpipe must be cut from the inside. It is largely done by feel; work both knife and free hand up the pipe to the highest point you can reach, and slice it through. Be careful of what your free hand is doing during the cutting operation.

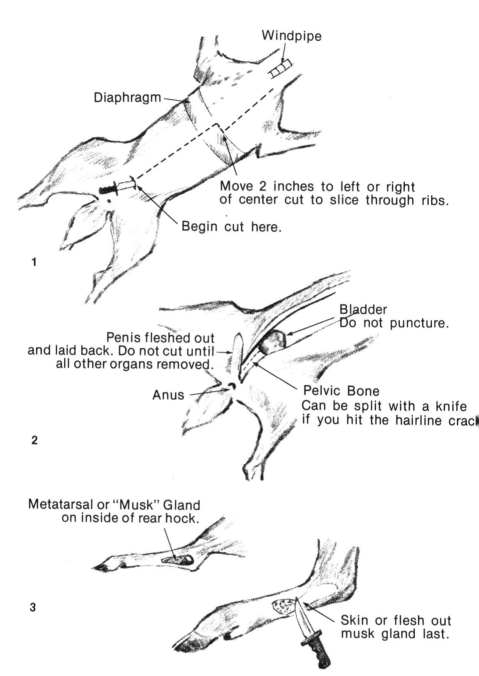

Windpipe

Diaphragm

Move 2 inches to left or right
of center cut to slice through ribs.

Begin cut here.

1

Penis fleshed out
and laid back. Do not cut until
all other organs removed.

Bladder
Do not puncture.

Anus

Pelvic Bone
Can be split with a knife
if you hit the hairline crack

2

Metatarsal or "Musk" Gland
on inside of rear hock.

3

Skin or flesh out
musk gland last.

1. *Initial gutting cut with location of the windpipe and diaphragm.*
2. *Fleshing out the genitals and pelvic bone.*
3. *Removing the musk gland.*

Removing attachments at the other end comes next. Flesh out the genitals as if you were skinning. On a doe, the teats can be removed and discarded. On a buck, the penis must be left whole until the bladder is removed, or you will end up with urine on the meat—another reason why some deer are "gamey." Flesh the penis out completely, working rearward to the point near the anus where it appears to enter the body, and lay it back.

Next, at the crotch where the two hind legs join, slice the meat cleanly and straight down until you hit bone. This will be the pelvis. At dead center, the pelvic bone has a hairline crack that runs its entire length; you can cut through that bone by inserting the knife point in the crack. You will probably have to hammer the handle of the knife with the heel of your hand to get the cut started, then lever the blade down to finish the break.

This pelvic-bone crack is a little tough to find if you haven't gutted many deer. You can also chop through the bone at any point near the middle by laying the edge of your knife near the crack, then gently striking the back of the knife with a fist-sized rock.

Once the bone is broken through, the terminal area of the small intestine will be exposed. Cut out the anus by fleshing it free from skin, bone, and the pelvic cavity.

If you are on an incline, now point the deer's head uphill. Grasp the windpipe and pull. Heart and lungs will come easily at first, along with the windpipe, then refuse to budge. Looking inside the cavity, you will note a fleshy wall of muscle that separates the respiratory from the digestive system. The wall is known as the diaphragm. Cut it free from the body cavity, and the remainder of the viscera can then be pulled from the carcass with little or no more cutting.

Removal of the metatarsal or "musk" gland is the last step. These swirls of foul-smelling hair, located on the inside hocks of the rear legs, are simply fleshed out. Always do this last so their odor won't be transferred to the meat by your knife blade. The job of "field dressing" is now complete.

Don't forget the heart and liver. The traditional menu for the night following a successful hunt is deer scrapple, and it is best made with these two organs.

Once you arrive back at camp with your deer, there is more cleaning to be done. Flush out the body cavity with water to remove blood and any hair or foreign material that might have gotten on the meat during the drag or dressing process. Thoroughly rinse any bloodshot areas, remove any and all fat you see, and pat exposed meat dry with a piece of cloth. When you are done, the body cavity should be spotless—the kind of meat you would expect to find in a butcher shop.

Cooling comes next, and this is a touchy matter because of variations in climate. In cold weather, there is no problem with meat spoilage from the heat, but early in the season and in the South, fresh-killed meat can go bad in a matter of hours.

Ideal cooling temperatures range from thirty-five to forty-five degrees. If the temperatures around camp average higher than that, you had better find a commercial cooler to hang your deer (most butcher shops have them). If temperatures are downright hot, get to the cooler in a hurry; don't wait for display and congratulations around camp—it could cost you your deer.

When hanging a deer, I prefer hoisting it up feet first. Because warm air rises, it will cool most quickly this way. If you hang it head first, some air is going to be trapped around the chest area, particularly if you are saving the head for a mount. Cooling will also be increased if you prop the chest cavity open with a stick to allow better circulation. It is wise to keep both hind feet level and wide apart, rather than hanging the carcass by one leg; it makes butchering a lot easier.

When to skin a deer. In colder climates, I prefer leaving the hide on the carcass until it is cured and time to butcher. I find that the meat stays moister and more flavorful that way. During

204

very warm weather, however, it is more important to cool the meat down in a hurry, so at this time I favor immediate removal of the hide.

When the carcass is still warm, no skinning method beats the golf-ball technique. For this method, you must hang the animal by its head.

Cut the hide in a circle around the deer's neck, then straight down the throat to a point between the animal's forelegs. Now make two more cuts at right angles, out and down the inside of the forelegs to the first joint. Circle both joints with cuts as you did the neck, and double-check all cuts to make sure they are completely through the skin.

Flesh out a patch of skin the size of a hand on the nape of the deer's neck, then take a golf ball (or equivalent-sized rock) and place it between the flesh and hide. Bunch the hide around the ball so it looks like a darning dummy inside a sock, then tie a stout rope around the hide surrounding the ball (the ball only provides a strong place to tie onto).

All that is left to do is to tie the rope to the bumper of a car or pickup truck, and drive away; the skin will peel as easily as if you were peeling a banana.

After meat cools and hangs for a while, the skin becomes more solidly affixed to the flesh and the golf-ball method is impossible. You will have to skin the deer by the conventional method, using a good skinning knife and elbow grease.

For this operation, the deer should be hung hind feet first. Begin with a cut on the inside of the hind leg where exposed meat begins, then work up and out to the first joint. Circle the joint, being careful not to cut through the hamstring (main tendon); it makes for an extremely handy handle when you have to move the meat.

Throughout the entire skinning process, the means of separating hide from flesh is the same: you pull on the hide with one hand, and with the other hand gently probe and slice with the

Golf-ball skinning. Skin out the neck and front shoulders so the hide can pull free. The golf ball simply provides a handle for the rope to wrap around. (An equal-sized rock will do.)

Georgia Department of Natural Resources

Tie onto the bumper of a pickup truck and back up.

Georgia Department of Natural Resources

The hide pulls free with the ease of peeling a banana.

blade of your knife. The skinning stroke isn't really a cutting motion, but rather a circular sweep of your wrist. At the same time as you are cutting, you should be twisting your knife slightly to aid in the separation.

Once one hind leg is skinned, do the other. When both flaps of leg hide are laid back from the flesh, the tail will appear to be rather solidly affixed to carcass and hide. It is, but you can cut through the joint at the base of the tail with ease, leaving the tail right on the skin.

The next step is the easiest part of skinning. Unless the hide is so cold as to be nearly frozen, it will peel from back and sides up to the withers with little or no knife work. Just get your back into it and force downward, peeling a section free at a time.

Some flesh from the flank may adhere to the hide about half-

207

way down. If you see meat appearing as you peel, get the hide/meat separation started again with your knife.

At the withers, the hide will again hang up, caught on the shoulders and forelegs. Skin the forelegs out just as you did the hind legs, slicing straight down the inside, then circling the first hock. Once the hide is over the forelegs, it will again peel easily until you get to the neck. Here, the hide is attached to the flesh quite solidly, and it has to be separated with a lot of knife work. Continue skinning until you reach the animal's head or the cut you made to remove the windpipe. Remove the head and hide from the carcass by first cutting the flesh with a knife, then slicing through the bone with a saw or cleaver.

This method of skinning is also perfectly suitable if you want to mount the head. Assuming that you opened the carcass just up to the brisket, there will be no cuts in the hide beyond the front shoulders, and this is just what a taxidermist needs to work with.

My advice at this point would be to wrap up the entire hide and head as one, and either freeze it or deliver it immediately to your taxidermist. Let him skin the head out rather than you. It's a delicate operation, and when it is done improperly a lot of extra work has to go into mounting. Because of this, most taxidermists prefer to tackle the little extra labor involved in pelting a head out themselves.

Aging

Personal tastes being what they are, it is misleading to say that aging will give you "better" deer meat. Aged and fresh meat will taste different: aged deer approaches beef; fresh deer is a little like veal. Aging also tenderizes meat. My tastes being what they are, I am for allowing meat to undergo some curing before butchering.

When it comes to how long, I use mold as a rule of thumb. The aging process allows bacteria to grow in the meat, and as it does, the bacteria adds flavor and breaks down the muscle fiber. One type of bacteria (or fungi) produces grayish-white spots of mold inside the body cavity after about a week of aging at forty degrees. When the mold begins to appear, I assume that it is time to butcher. (The mold is easily washed off with a weak vinegar/water solution.)

Preparation of the Carcass

Before butchering, go over the carcass with a fine-tooth comb and a washrag which has been dipped into a weak vinegar/water solution. This final bath removes any residue blood and hair that might flavor the meat during long periods in a freezer.

Trim off all fat from the animal. Deer fat in itself doesn't taste bad, but it is likely to pick up objectionable odors from a freezer, and also freezer-burns more easily than meat.

You should also trim off any dry, excess meat, particularly the thin stomach flank between ribs and haunch, and the flaps of flesh that surrounded the windpipe on the neck.

Pay particular attention to the meat surrounding the point of bullet entry. Remove and discard any flesh that isn't clean and firm and free of clotted blood.

Butchering

Even though you have never tried butchering before, I would recommend cutting up your own deer unless you know a pro you can trust. Since passage of the new meat and butchering standards laws a few years back, wild game must be processed in a room separate from that used for processing domestic meats for public sale.

This usually means that big-game carcasses are butchered en masse on one or two days a week set aside during the hunting season. By honest human error, you could conceivably end up with someone else's meat—someone who didn't take care of his deer as well as you. Then, too, the tools used to butcher animal after animal are bound to carry some unwanted flavor, and a common way of making hamburger is to throw all scraps in a common pot, then divvy up the meat in equal shares after it goes through the grinder. That can result in some "gamy" meat.

Butchery isn't difficult, especially if you have the correct tools. A boning knife 6 to 8 inches long, a butcher knife 14 to 18 inches long, and a meat cleaver are of paramount importance. These can be bought at hardware stores and should be kept razor sharp.

A meat saw is a big help, but a little more difficult to come by. Hardware stores occasionally carry them, and you may be able to buy a used saw from the local butcher. Fine-toothed wood saws will do in a pinch, but you will have to resharpen them after they have been used on bone.

My final tool for butchering is a bit uncommon: a hand power saw, with the blade reversed. More about it and its use in a moment.

The biggest mistake made in butchering a deer occurs when you try to superimpose diagrams and road maps of the cuts that come from other animals: hogs, sheep, and especially beef. A deer is a deer, and it is cut up in a way special to its kind.

Begin with the carcass hanging upside down. Using the meat saw, trim off the legs just below the knee joints. Next, cut the carcass in half. If you will stand facing the animal's back, you will even have a line to follow—one that runs right down the middle of its back.

As you cut, it may help to have someone steady the carcass, since it will begin to swing in time with your arm. It is also quite important to keep the blade sawing at dead center. If you find yourself going off to one side or the other, guide the blade back in place by twisting it in the proper direction with your free hand while you cut gently with the other.

Keep cutting down the center line until you reach the point where the shoulder joins the neck. Here, make a right-angle

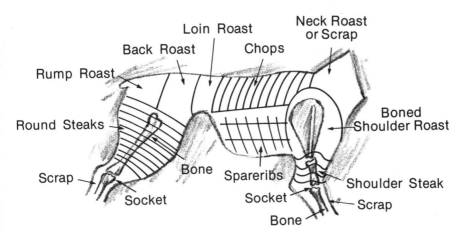

Cuts on a carcass

turn to the left or right, separating the two halves of deer and allowing the neck to remain whole.

Cut up each half-deer further into three large pieces: the shoulder, ribs, and haunch. Then butcher these pieces individually. It is much easier to handle the meat this way.

Remove the shoulder from the carcass by grasping the foreleg and pulling it away from the ribs. Begin cutting at the arm (leg?) pit on the inside of the foreleg where it joins the body. Using the butcher knife, slice upward toward the back, using long, firm strokes that guide the knife close to the ribs. You will find the entire shoulder peeling off without your having to cut through bone. The cut will be complete, and the shoulder free from the rest of the carcass, when you slice through the muscle at the top of the withers—roughly the place where the shoulders, neck, and back meet.

The shoulder will produce three cuts of meat. Stew meat or hamburger lies between the end of the foreleg and the first joint. Remove this meat by slicing it free with a boning knife. Steaks come from the meaty area just above the first joint. Slice them crosswise and about an inch thick with the butcher knife, then cut them free of the heavy leg bone with your boning knife. On a medium-sized deer, you should be able to get four small steaks from each shoulder. Unless you are quite practiced in meat cutting, you are not going to be able to cut shoulder steaks so cleanly that there is no meat left on the leg bone. Remove these scraps with a boning knife and include them with the hamburger and stew meat.

The blade will now be all that is left of the shoulder. Lay it on your worktable outside up and test the meat with your thumb. You will find a straight, narrow ridge of bone just under the skin that runs the length of the shoulder blade. Take your boning knife and slice down into the meat on each side of the ridge for its full length.

With the thumb and forefinger of one hand, pull the meat away from the ridge and begin to separate the meat from the bone with the boning knife. The stroke is much like the circular motion used for skinning. Go full around the shoulder blade so you end up with what is essentially a sheet of meat, and a boned and cleaned shoulder blade.

Roll up the meat as you would a newspaper, and tie it with stout cotton string in at least three places. You now have a boned, rolled shoulder roast, and have butchered out the shoulder.

The ribs and back are next. With saw or cleaver, cut them free from the haunch at the loins—the narrowest part of the deer's back, just in front of the haunch. Lay this part of the carcass inside down on your worktable.

Butcher the ribs by imagining three cutting lines parallel to each other and 4 to 6 inches apart, running at right angles to the ribs. To cut them, you can use a cleaver, a handsaw, or, quicker yet, the power saw. Start with a cut close to the brisket, then two more successively closer to the back. Don't cut into the thick meat of the back; this area starts about 9 inches below the top of the back and should be saved for chops.

The strips of ribs you get will look a little like a ladder. Cut them into square pieces with a knife. The cartilaginous brisket bones can be cut with a cleaver.

Obviously, the butchered ribs are for spareribs. If for some reason, you don't care for spareribs, you can make just one cut close to the back to separate the ribs from the rest of the carcass, then bone out the rib flesh with a knife. The meat can be used for hamburger or stew and is ideal for jerky.

You are now confronted with a long strip of meat and bone— one half of the entire backbone. Lay it so that the ribs face you, the top of the back faces away from you, and the cut you made with the saw to separate the two halves rests on the table.

The meat which lies between the cut end in the loin area and the first rib is all roast. If you want one large roast, call it a back roast. If you want two smaller roasts, call the first cut a loin roast, the second one a back roast. Cut through the meat with a butcher knife first, then through the bone with the handsaw.

The rib area produces chops. Using the butcher knife, cut through the meat that rests between the ribs, one clean cut between each rib. Slice so that the cut goes perfectly between and absolutely parallel to each rib. Now, lay your cleaver in that cut so that it rests against the bone of the back. Tap the top of the cleaver with a hammer (preferably a wooden mallet), and perfect chops will slough off.

As you move forward toward the neck, chops will become less well defined around the area of the withers. Bone this meat out for stew or hamburger. The neck can be a roast, or it can be boned out for scraps.

The haunch is the last piece to cut up. As with the foreleg, use the meat lying between the end of the leg and the first joint as scrap. The rear leg joint is a massive, bony thing, so rather than cutting it right at the joint, use the handsaw just above it.

The haunch meat can be used for a great roast as it is (it makes for a distinctive outdoor barbecue), it can be smoked, or it can be

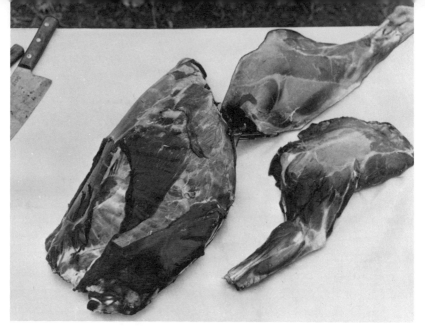

Each half carcass is cut into three pieces for easy handling: ribs (largest piece), shoulder (lower leg), and haunch or hindquarter (upper leg).

The shoulder meat is boned from the shoulderblade, then rolled into a roast.

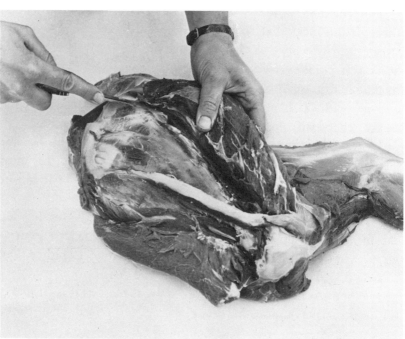

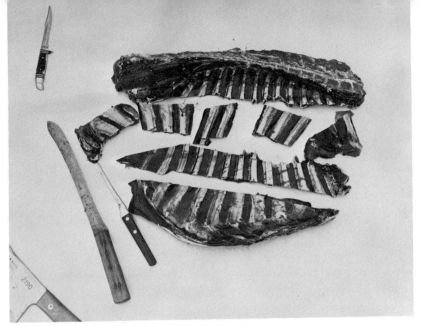

Ribs are cut into squares; the back provides roasts and chops.

Cut between the ribs, then cleave them apart; the results are meat as attractive as you might find in any butcher shop.

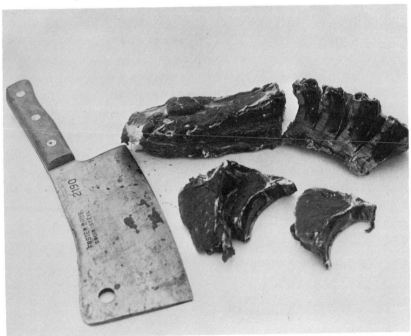

cut into roasts and steaks. Out of my three deer a year, I usually smoke one haunch, save one haunch for a summer barbecue, and cut the rest up into steaks.

The trick to cutting good-looking steaks is a sharp knife and a clean stroke. Starting 1 to 1½ inches above the joint cut, and parallel to that cut, draw the butcher knife from hilt to point in one motion, bearing down moderately hard. This should bring you right down to the leg bone. Saw the bone with the power saw. The handsaw is extremely difficult to use on a leg because the bone moves with your arm and binds the saw. One more hilt-to-point stroke should sever the rest of the meat and give you a professional-looking steak that any butcher would be proud to call his own.

Continue cutting steaks from the haunch 1 to 1½ inches thick. You should get between six and eight steaks, then run into the second joint. Here the hind leg meets the pelvic bone, and further steak cuts are impossible. Use the chunk of meat remaining as a rump roast. If it's too large for your purposes, you can cut it in half at right angles to the back, calling one half a rump, the other a back roast.

Wrapping

Freezer burn is a common cause of poor-tasting deer meat. It can be avoided if you will double-wrap your meat in commercial butcher paper. When wrapping, do it tightly, making sure that there are no air spaces inside the package; contact of air with meat is a primary cause of freezer burn.

Secure the wrap with masking tape, and mark the package with a grease pencil as to the nature of the cut and the number of people the meat will feed. It is also a good idea to mark the year. Using this method, we keep deer meat frozen all year long and find the meat of excellent flavor whenever we eat it.

Recipes

Too many people make the mistake of expecting deer to taste

like beef, then are disappointed when it doesn't. It is unfortunate —and a little ridiculous. After all, turning thumbs down on a prime pork roast or leg of lamb because it doesn't taste like a T-bone steak hardly makes much sense, yet that is essentially much of the criticism leveled at venison.

Deer is deer, with a unique flavor all its own, so if you have never tried it before, be prepared for a new taste and judge it on its own merits.

Although the flavor of deer can't really be compared with that of beef, the cooking of it can. Virtually any recipe that calls for beef can be used for venison: soups, steaks, roasts, stews, and more. If you like your beef rare, chances are that you will like your deer cooked the same way. The old rule that wild meat of any kind should always be cooked thoroughly is dead wrong, and often a good way to ruin some excellent eating.

While virtually every conceivable recipe for venison has been tried in our kitchen up Cottonwood Canyon or in deer camp, there are some favorites we lean on heavily. Our enjoyment of them has been so great that they are listed here for yours.

Deer Hamburger

At one time we saved all our meat scraps for stews. Deer hamburger was just too dry for our tastes. Then Dave Wolny showed up one evening with a meat grinder and his method of making hamburger, and we did an about-face. These hamburgers are especially delicious cooked over a charcoal grill.

1½ pounds beef suet
5 pounds deer scraps
1 clove garlic, finely minced

Cut the suet and deer into 2-inch pieces. Put the suet and deer pieces through a meat grinder. Run the ground meat through the grinder again, adding the minced garlic to the mixture. Freeze either into patties or packages that suit the size of your family.

217

Jerky and Pemmican

Deer was a primary food for the American Indian, who devised a way to preserve the meat for years without refrigeration. Jerky and pemmican are high-energy foods that weigh little but make for quite a meal when mixed with a drink of water.

They are perfect—and uniquely appropriate—food for the deer hunter on the trail, since several meals can be carried in your pocket. At home, served with beer, they make for party snacks that beat peanuts and potato chips by a wilderness mile.

Jerky

4 pounds meat cut into pieces approximately 1″ × 2″ × 8″
2 teaspoons salt
4 teaspoons powdered barbecue seasoning
2 teaspoons chili pepper and curry powder mixture (optional)

Cut away all fat, gristle, and tendon from the strips of meat. Combine the seasonings in a saltshaker. Pound the meat with a meat hammer and, as you pound, sprinkle with the seasonings. (There should be about ¼ teaspoon of the combination spread across each side of each strip of meat.)

Place the strips directly on the oven rack, turn the gauge to 150° F., and leave them there until all the moisture is gone, usually about 7 hours. The strips should feel like dry leather when done and should be supple enough to bend a little without breaking.

Pemmican

3 to 4 cups jerky pieces
½ pint dried chopped fruit (raisins are fine but anything works)
¼ pint chopped nuts
¼ pint hot animal fat (preferably beef or pork as wild fat absorbs foreign odors)

Powder the jerky by pounding with a clean hammer until you have 1 pint that looks like dried hamburger. Add the remaining ingredients and mix well. Before the mixture fully cools, shape into golf-sized balls. The fat will harden and the pemmican will keep its shape. Pemmican doesn't keep as well or as long as jerky, since the fat sours after a while (about a month in the relatively cool Montana summer), but it is ideal for the average high mountain camping trip. Like jerky, it can be eaten as is (one ball to a meal) or cooked in soups or stews.

Scrapple

Whenever a deer is brought into camp, tradition demands that scrapple be served that night. Scrapple is also excellent for breakfast, served with eggs.

4   cups beef bouillon
1   cup cornmeal
1   teaspoon salt
1½ pounds finely chopped deer liver
½   pound finely chopped deer heart
1   onion, finely chopped
¼   pound butter or margarine
½   cup flour
3   tablespoons butter or margarine

Bring the bouillon to a rapid boil and slowly add the cornmeal. Stir constantly until the mixture returns to a boil. Add the salt, reduce the heat, cover, and cook slowly for 5 to 7 minutes.

Fry the chopped deer liver, heart, and onions in butter, stirring frequently, until the meat is an even color (5 to 7 minutes). Stir into the cornmeal. Pour the mixture into a shallow baking pan and chill until it becomes firm.

Slice the scrapple into ¼-inch slices, roll in flour, and fry in butter until both sides are golden brown. Serves 4.

Spareribs

People often discard deer ribs or save them for dog food. That is a big mistake. Deer spareribs are meaty, lean, and delicious, attested to by the fact that it is the packages of ribs that usually disappear from our freezer first.

> 3 tablespoons bacon fat
> Salt and pepper to taste
> 3 pounds deer ribs
> ½ cup brown sugar
> 2 cups barbecue sauce

Melt the bacon fat in a heavy skillet. Salt and pepper the ribs and brown them in the bacon fat. Place in a 9-by-12-inch roasting pan and sprinkle half the brown sugar on the ribs. Pour the barbecue sauce over the ribs and top with the rest of the brown sugar.* Bake at 375° F. for 2 hours or until done.

Spiced Deer and Dumplings

Here's a meal that is perfectly suited to large roasts and lots of company for dinner. It is also a good recipe for meat you deem to have an objectionable taste. The spices and long cooking cover up distinct flavor characteristics to a point where deer is indistinguishable from other meats.

> 3- to 4-pound deer roast
> 4 tablespoons bacon fat
> 1 1-pound can tomatoes (2 cups)
> ¼ cup wine vinegar
> ½ cup water
> 1 clove garlic, minced
> 7 whole cloves
> ¾ teaspoon mixed pickling spice
> 1 teaspoon salt
> ½ teaspoon pepper
> 1 package refrigerated biscuits
> 1 tablespoon parsley

Trim any fat from the roast. Heat the bacon fat in a large Dutch oven. Slowly brown the meat on all sides in the hot fat. Add the next 8 ingredients. Cover; cook slowly for 2 to 3 hours

---

* This combination of barbecue sauce and brown sugar is also quite delicious when painted on roasts, chops, and steaks cooked over charcoal on a grill.

or until tender. Place the biscuits on the meat; sprinkle with the parsley. Cover tightly and steam 10 to 15 minutes or until the "dumplings" are done. Remove the meat and dumplings to a warm platter. Make gravy using 2 tablespoons flour and ¼ cup cold water. (Add the water to the meat stock to make 1½ cups.)

Scallopini

When you are tired of stews, try this unusual way to prepare, cook, and eat deer scraps.

    2 pounds meat
    ½ cup all-purpose flour
    2 tablespoons paprika
    ½ teaspoon salt
    ¼ teaspoon pepper
    3 tablespoons fat
    1 4-ounce can mushrooms
    1 bouillon cube
    1 8-ounce can tomato sauce
    ¼ cup chopped green peppers
    ½ cup red table wine
      Grated Parmesan cheese

Tenderize the meat thoroughly by pounding with a mallet and cut into bite-size pieces. Combine the flour, paprika, salt, and pepper and dredge the meat in the mixture. Heat the fat until it starts to sizzle but not smoke. Brown the meat in the hot fat, then remove to a baking dish.

Drain the canned mushrooms, add water to the liquid to make 1 cup, and heat until it boils. Dissolve the bouillon cube in the mushroom liquid and pour over the meat. Bake in a 350° oven for 45 minutes.

Combine the tomato sauce, green peppers, mushrooms, and wine in a saucepan and simmer for 30 minutes while the meat is baking. Pour over the meat during the last 15 minutes of baking time and baste with the sauce once or twice. Serve with noodles and sprinkle with grated Parmesan cheese. Serves 6.

Deer Hunting

Breaded Chops

Chops are the most tender cut of meat on a deer, and breading them is our favorite way to prepare them. Breading not only adds a delicate flavor; it seals in juices and helps preserve tenderness.

1 beaten egg
½ cup milk
8 ¾-inch deer chops
1 cup Italian-flavored bread crumbs
½ stick of margarine
Salt and pepper to taste

Mix the egg and milk. Dip the meat in the egg mixture, then in the crumbs. Brown on both sides in the margarine, season with salt and pepper, and cook until done to your taste; we like them pink-rare. Serves 4.

Seared Deer Steaks

This isn't really a recipe—just a technique. The next time you cook a deer steak over coals, heat a heavy iron skillet until it sweats. Drop the steak in; it should crackle, sizzle, and sear. After 15 to 30 seconds, turn the steak and sear the other side. Now cook it over open coals as you normally would, turning the meat with a spatula, not a fork. You will enjoy juicy, tender, and flavorful meat that defies description.

Sil's Stew

Of all the exotic recipes we enjoy, we have to admit that an honest stew is hard to beat for flavor. Cook it up in the morning, then leave the pot simmering all day long. This is a particularly good dish around camp, since hunters can straggle in anytime they want and still enjoy a fresh, hot meal. Don't let them finish it all, though; save some for yourself tomorrow. Stew always tastes better the second day.

2 pounds deer, cut into 1-inch cubes
2 tablespoons fat
1 28-ounce can tomatoes
4 cups boiling water
1 tablespoon lemon juice
1 tablespoon Worcestershire sauce
1 tablespoon soy sauce
1 clove garlic
1 medium onion, sliced
2 bay leaves
1 tablespoon salt
1 teaspoon sugar
1 beef bouillon cube
½ teaspoon pepper
½ teaspoon paprika
⅛ teaspoon allspice or cloves

3 large potatoes, diced
1 can peas, drained
6 carrots, sliced
1 can string beans, drained

Thoroughly brown the deer on all sides in the hot fat. Add the tomatoes, water, lemon juice, Worcestershire sauce, soy sauce, garlic, onion, bay leaves, salt, sugar, bouillon cube, and spices. Cover, then simmer, but don't boil, for 2 hours, stirring occasionally to keep from sticking. Remove the bay leaves.

Add the potatoes, peas, carrots, and string beans. Cook for 30 minutes more, or until the vegetables are done. The liquid can be thickened with flour, if desired. Serves 8 or more.

Shepherd's Stew

This is an ideal meal for an outback camp, short on conveniences. It requires little preparation and fewer skills, and because it is cooked in aluminum foil, there is no cleanup afterward.

½ pound diced wild meat (substitute hamburger or other ground
  meat)
1 small carrot, cut into thin slices
1 small potato, cut into thin slices
½ teaspoon dried minced onion
1 square foot heavy aluminum foil
  Salt and pepper to taste
1 bouillon cube dissolved in ½ cup hot water

Combine the meat, sliced carrots and potatoes and minced
onion in the center of the square of foil and sprinkle with the
seasonings. Pour the broth over the mixture, fold the foil around
it, seal, leaving some space for steam expansion, and bury the
package in coals. Cook 20 to 30 minutes in a hot fire.

Pour the juices into a cup and drink as a hot broth. Eat the
stew directly out of the foil package.

Shish Kebabs

This Middle East dish requires little preparation and nothing
of the cook, and involves minimal cleanup afterward. It is ideal
for camp or an outdoor barbecue, and a bit unusual since individual diners have the opportunity to become their own crea-
tive cooks. Provide as much of these ingredients as you think your
crowd will eat.

Sliced bacon, cut in half and folded
Whole mushroom caps, lightly cooked in butter
Onion chunks
Small potatoes, cooked
Green pepper chunks
Tomato slices
1½-inch chunks of venison
Salt and pepper to taste
Butter or barbecue sauce

Assemble kebabs by alternating the bacon, mushrooms,
onions, potatoes, peppers, tomatoes, and meat on 12- to 24-inch
skewers. Grill over coals until done. Baste with either a butter

sauce or your favorite barbecue sauce. To serve: rest the end of the skewer on a plate and push the food off the skewer with a knife.

For extra flavor, marinate the meat before cooking in Soy Marinade and use the marinade for basting as the kebabs are grilled.

Soy Marinade

¾ cup soy sauce
½ cup red wine
1 tablespoon curry powder
¼ teaspoon powdered ginger
1 clove minced garlic

Combine the ingredients. Pour over boneless cubes of meat and let stand overnight in a refrigerator or cooler.

Sauerbraten

This is a rich, delicious German meal that can feed from four to forty. It is best when prepared with stew meat, and is an excellent way to cook venison that has picked up an objectionable flavor. Like stew, sauerbraten tastes even better the second day.

2 tablespoons sugar
2 cups vinegar
2 cups water
2 medium onions
1 sliced lemon
3 bay leaves
10 peppercorns
10 whole cloves
2 tablespoons salt
4 pounds meat
½ cup flour
2 tablespoons cooking oil

Combine all the ingredients except the meat, flour, and cooking oil in a large dish. (Don't use metal.) Bone and dice the meat into 2-inch-square pieces and marinate in the mixture for at least 36 hours. Stir at least once a day.

Remove the meat from the liquid, dry with a towel, and dredge in flour. Brown all sides of the meat in the cooking oil for about 20 minutes. Strain the marinade and add 2 cups of the liquid to the browned meat. Cover and cook over very low heat for 3 to 4 hours or until it is so tender that it literally falls apart.

Use the cooking liquid as a base for thick, brown gravy and serve over dumplings with red cabbage and black bread. Serves 8 to 12.

Horns, Hooves, and Hides

In the days when America was Indian country and the Ohio River a frontier, deer provided the hunter with a lot more than just meat. Bones and horns were used for needles and fishhooks, sinew was used for thread, horns were fashioned into tools, and hides were used for clothes and cookware.

Historic handicrafts aside, the current practicality of some of these goods is questionable; steel fishhooks and needles are more efficient than bone, and people no longer boil water by dropping fire-heated rocks into a leathern vessel. There are still, however, many items which are useful and aesthetic by today's standards that can be made from those parts of a deer carcass that are all too often discarded. And making and using them will account for a pride of ownership that goes beyond mere possession.

There is something uniquely appropriate about a hunting knife with a handle fashioned from the horn of a deer you shot, or a buckskin shirt with bone buttons that you wear while hunting. Part of the pleasure is surely the attachment of memories, but there is a symbolism involved too. In the total use of a deer—hide, horns, hooves, and meat—there is evident the kind of symbiosis that is the keynote of nature.

HORNS are most commonly used as a display in rec room or den. There, they can double as a hat or gun rack.

Hooves, horns, and hides all have uses: A buckskin shirt is the most comfortable clothing to ever grace your back. Hooves make excellent gun racks and clothes hangers, and horns can be fashioned into knife handles, buttons, clasps, and drawstring ends.

To mount horns, cut them, still attached to the skullcap, free of the deer's head with a meat saw. It is important to keep the skullcap and horns in one piece, since it makes the mounting job infinitely easier.

Once the cap and horns are free of the skull, remove the hide and hair from the cap with a small knife. Since the work is rather delicate, a small hunting or pocket knife is better for this job than a skinning knife.

When the hide is off, small amounts of meat will still cling to the bone. This is most easily removed by boiling the bone in water for ten minutes.

There are two ways horns are mounted on a plaque: with a velvet or felt covering over the white bone, or with the bone left exposed. Generally, the velvet is used on a mount that will hang inside a house, and the bone is left exposed on horns that will be tacked to a garage, over a door, or under the eaves of a hunting cabin.

On both types of mounts, two holes for mounting screws should be predrilled through the skullcap. A small speed drill does this job most efficiently. For a velvet mount, a wooden backplate (½-inch plywood is best) must be fashioned, slightly smaller than the dimensions of the skullcap. The horns are then fastened to this plate with screws.

Stretch the velvet across the bone on top of a thin padding of foam rubber, then tack it in place behind the cap on the wooden plate with carpet or upholstery tacks.

Predrill two more holes through the final mounting plaque, and screw from the back into the wooden plate.

Exposed-bone mounts can be screwed into a plaque or a wall directly from the front. If your horns are to hang outside, cover them with a coat of top-grade exterior varnish or they will bleach and deteriorate. Interior mounts don't require varnish since they won't be exposed to the elements.

Occasionally, hunters and hikers find horns that have been

kicked or sometimes knocked off by a shedding buck. It is rare to find a matched set since both horns aren't dropped simultaneously, but matched sets aren't necessary to make attractive gun, hat, and clothes racks.

To mount a single horn, drill directly into the base of the antler with a ¼-inch speed drill, to a depth of about an inch. Insert a ¼-inch hardwood dowel and glue it in place with epoxy glue. You can then mount the horn by drilling one more ¼-inch hole in the plaque or wall, cutting the dowel to fit, and gluing it there.

There are dozens of other items you can make with horns—or parts of them. A few examples would include:

• Buttons and jewelry, made by cutting antlers crosswise with a hacksaw, then polishing them. Polish first with light sandpaper, next with steel wool of coarse, medium, and light grade in that order. Finish the job with pumice stone and then rotten stone. The effect will be a glass-smooth and shiny surface with a depth that reflects several circular shades of color. Use the thick base of the antler for brooches, bolo ties, money clips, and belt buckles. Antler material glues tight to metal with epoxy, and will stick best if you finish the surface to be glued with sandpaper only.

Use the thin antler-tip section of horn for buttons. They are easiest to polish if you smooth the antler end while it is still whole (you then have something to hold onto). Cut the antler with a hacksaw and use the polished side for the front of the button. Drill buttonholes with a tiny speed drill (¹⁄₁₆ or ³⁄₃₂ of an inch in diameter).

• The very tip of an antler makes handsome ends for drawstrings, lamp chains, and zipper pulls. Drill directly into the base of a 1- to 2-inch antler tip, then insert the rawhide, bead chain, or whatever. Glue it in place with epoxy.

• Large pieces of antler make beautiful handles for hunting knives and kitchen cutlery. This generally involves drilling through the center of the antler, then gluing the shaft of the knife in place. Antler material can be shaped with a fine wood rasp to conform to a hilt or metal butt, then polished as you would for a brooch or a button. Antler material can also be cut in longitudinal slabs with a hacksaw to make handles for pocket knives, trim for draw handles, decoration on lighters, etc.

Hooves, too, can be used for gun, clothes, and hat racks.

After the legs have been severed for butchering, inject taxidermists' curing compound into any meaty area or joint with a hypodermic needle, then block the legs up so the hoof is at right angles to the first joint. Leave the legs in that position until they get hard—about a month.

Once the legs are thoroughly dry and rock-hard, it is time for mounting. Legs should be mounted on a long, finished 1 x 4, pointing at right angles to the board, for a coat or hat rack. For a gun rack, they are mounted on two 1 x 4s, two to a board, and in line with the board's longest dimension.

Decide how far you wish the feet to protrude from the mounting plaque. If the rack is to hold four guns, you will have to leave enough space for them to fit two deep. If two guns are all they will hold, the spread between plaque and hoof should be narrow enough to hold them fast in an upright position.

Once you have determined the proper measurement, cut the leg bones with a hacksaw, leaving an extra ¾ inch of bone. This bone acts like a dowel. Trim the hide and hair clean from the last ¾ inch of leg with a sharp knife, then round the bone with a fine rasp. Drill an appropriate-sized hole into the mounting plaque with a wood bit, insert the legs, and glue them into position with epoxy.

DEER HIDE is one of the softest, most pleasant-to-wear clothing materials you will ever have on your back. What is more, buckskin is extremely attractive, with a soft, earthy-looking texture that is as pleasant to the eye as it is to the touch, explaining in part the $150 price tag that accompanies a buckskin jacket—if you can find one at all.

Unlike horns and hooves, however, hides require quite a bit of preparation before you can make something useful out of them. The process is called tanning.

Tanning involves chemicals, special tools, and elbow grease. First, all fats and flesh must be removed from the inside of the hide with a fleshing tool or knife; then the hair is removed from the outside by soaking the skin in a strong chemical. The hide is further treated with a pickling solution, then allowed to dry.

Once it is dry, the real work begins—long hours spent kneading and working the stiff hide into live, leathery softness over a "fleshing beam," a piece of cut hardwood resembling an ironing board.

Tanning is an art unto itself, and if you are interested in tackling it, you will need more information than can be justified here. Herter's Inc., R.R. 1, Waseca, Minnesota, supplies equipment, chemicals, and a book on how to do it. The basic kit is around $15.

In lieu of tanning a hide yourself, you can have the job done by a tannery. Note, I said tannery, not taxidermist. Taxidermists, because most of their work is done by hand, charge plenty to tan a hide. Tanneries, with their mass production and machinery, should do a hide for between six and eight dollars, depending on its size.

Tanneries are usually listed in the classified section of sports magazines. Taxidermists will also be glad to tell you the addresses of tanneries they use. Pick the tannery closest to your home; unless you are lucky and have one in town, you must send your hide through the mail, and the Post Office is understandably disturbed when they have to handle packages that smell. Your hide will have an odor if it has been in a heated room for a few days.

To send a hide, salt the flesh side thoroughly with low-grade commercial salt, roll it up, and leave it overnight. The salt will remove much of the water and fat in the hide by absorption. It will "leak"—produce a fluid—so don't leave it on your living room floor.

Next, thoroughly cover the flesh side with borax. The stuff used for washing is fine. This, too, absorbs moisture and cuts down on odor while in transit. Box the hide up and send it off.

Deer hides can be used to make buckskin shirts and jackets, vests, gloves, moccasins, handbags, and more. Assuming that you are of medium to large build, you will need four large skins for a jacket, three for a shirt, and two for a vest. Gloves, moccasins, and handbags can be made from the scraps you cut from these skins.

Patterns, available from sewing shops, are necessary. So is a little savvy, for working with deerskin isn't quite the same as sewing cloth.

You must orient the pattern the same way as the skin. The neck of a shirt would be at the neck end of the hide. When cutting, cut from neck to butt; this is the way the grain runs.

You will need a top-grade sewing machine with a powerful motor (the better home models are strong enough), and a ready supply of needles sharp enough to drive through the leather.

Silk thread, because it is strong, slippery, and doesn't cut the leather, is best for sewing. Because the fabric is so thick, use larger stitching than for cloth.

Tacking or pinning seams in excess of what would be normal for cloth is necessary. Deerskin stretches quite a bit, and unless you have a tack every few inches, you will end up with a bunch of hide or unequal lengths at the end of a seam. The job of tacking will be a lot easier if you use staples instead of pins.

Seams wear best when they overlap. They will lie flat, and they are also easier to sew.

In lieu of sewing, you can glue a buckskin shirt together with shoemaker's cement. Barge Cement is one brand name I have used with satisfactory results. It is a contact-type cement that remains supple when it sets up.

To use this stuff, you carefully paint it on both faces to be joined, then let it dry until it gets tacky. Mate up the seam perfectly before pressing the two pieces together. Once the contact is made, the bond is for keeps.

Seams, collars, and cuffs that don't want to lie perfectly flat can be beaten into submission with a leather mallet. The use of a mallet on a glued seam is a good idea anyway, since it ensures full contact and a better bond.

Epilogue

Today is October 15, 1972. It's 4:00 p.m., and my den is sour with the smell of smoke. I smoke way too much when I write, my wife tells me.

But that will be corrected—the book is done. And I'll have to pay the piper for all those forbidden butts in a very few days. The leaves have turned golden and are beginning to fall. Another deer season is nearly here, and next Sunday will dawn brightly with me huffing my way up the mountain behind my cabin. A very unusual mountain, I might add; most of them wear down with time, but this one keeps getting taller.

Finishing a book, especially this one, is a time of mixed emotions. On the one hand, you are glad it's over, that your effort is finished and complete. On the other hand, you are sorry there is no more to it, for there is great fun in the doing and the telling and the learning. There are some parallels that exist with downing a fine buck, or sundown on the last day of deer season. You are always glad it's over, but wouldn't it be great to go through it just one more time?

So I reflect on what I have said and what I felt, and I suddenly realize that a kind of catharsis has taken place. In the nuts and bolts of putting words and ideas and information on paper,

235

I have learned a great deal—about hunting and hunters, deer and nature, even myself—that I somehow wasn't quite so aware of before I began this book. And I also realize that I have enjoyed the process immensely.

My consummate hope is that others will do likewise.

North Dakota Game and Fish Department

The End

Bibliography

Laycock, George, *The Deer Hunter's Bible* (Doubleday, 1963).

Linsdale, Jean M., & Tomich, P. Quentin, *A Herd of Mule Deer* (University of California Press, 1953).

Mattis, George, *Whitetail* (World Publications Co., 1969).

Mussehl, Thomas W., & Howell, F. W., eds. *Game Management in Montana* (Montana Fish and Game Department, 1971).

Rue, Leonard Lee III, *The World of the Whitetail Deer* (J. B. Lippincott, 1962).

Russo, John P., *The Kaibab North Deer Herd* (Arizona Fish & Game Department, 1964).

Taylor, Walter P., ed. *The Deer of North America* (Stackpole Books, 1956).

Teer, James G., *Texas Deer Herd Management*, Bulletin 44 (Texas Parks and Wildlife Department, 1963).

Tillet, Paul, *Doe Day* (Rutgers University Press, 1963).

Vermont's Game Annual (Vermont Fish and Game Department, 1962–1972).